How Does a Daughter Survive the Loss of a Mother's Love?

"More than a decade after my mother's death, I still converse with her."

"As my mother told me one day before she went into the hospital for the first time, 'You may not always hear me, but you'll always feel my answer.'"

"I'd learned to express my love for her whenever I felt it. I didn't need to see my mother's body for closure. . . . I chose instead to live with the memories of my mother full of life, and not without it."

"The closer I get to her age [at death], the clearer it becomes to me that we each were given our own paths to walk in life. Believing in this gives me huge amounts of freedom and joy."

OTHER BOOKS BY HOPE EDELMAN

Motherless Daughters
Motherless Mothers
Mother of My Mother
The Possibility of Everything
Boys Like That

LETTERS FROM

Motherless Daughters

Words of Courage, Grief, and Healing

Edited and with an Introduction by

Hope Edelman

Da Capo
LIFE
LONG

A MEMBER OF THE PERSEUS BOOKS GROUP

Copyright © 2014 by Hope Edelman

For information, address Da Capo Press, 44 Farnsworth Street, 3rd Floor,
Boston, MA 02210

Designed by Jack Lenzo
Set in 12 point Garamond by the Perseus Books Group

Cataloging-in-Publication data for this book is available from the Library
of Congress.

First Da Capo Press edition 2014
ISBN: 978-0-7382-1753-6 (paperback)
ISBN: 978-0-7382-1754-3 (e-book)

Published by Da Capo Press
A Member of the Perseus Books Group
www.dacapopress.com

Da Capo Press books are available at special discounts for bulk purchases
in the U.S. by corporations, institutions, and other organizations. For more
information, please contact the Special Markets Department at the Perseus
Books Group, 2300 Chestnut Street, Suite 200, Philadelphia, PA, 19103, or call
(800) 810-4145, ext. 5000, or e-mail special.markets@perseusbooks.com.

For my Aunt Rosalie, who is deeply missed

Contents

Acknowledgments

To Elizabeth Kaplan, my agent, for twenty years of excellent advice and support; my editor Renée Sedliar and the team at Perscus, for believing in the enduring power of this book; Wendy Hudson, for invaluable assistance in all matters Internet and editorial; Belen Ricoy, for loving my daughters almost as much as I do; Hedgebrook women's writing retreat, for time and space and radical hospitality; Maya and Eden, for making every day a new adventure; and Uzi, for everything else and more: thank you. So much.

Preface

In the letters, e-mails, and phone calls I received after the publication of *Motherless Daughters*, many of the women who'd read the book asked for more. They wanted more stories from other women who'd lost their mothers, more information about the grieving process, and further assurance that their experiences were neither isolated nor unique. Hundreds of women sent me their personal stories of mother loss, and many of them generously agreed to participate in a subsequent book.

Letters from Motherless Daughters was compiled in 1995 to fulfill these requests. Even after its publication, the letters kept coming in, first via regular mail and then over the Internet. Nearly twenty years later, I still receive e-mails and Facebook messages every day from readers all over the world, many from teenage girls whose losses are recent and raw. This twentieth anniversary edition includes thirty-four of the original letters and nineteen new ones. That it is impossible to distinguish between past letters and new ones is testimony to the universal and timeless nature of grief.

The women whose letters appear in this book come from all over the United States as well as Canada, Australia, and the United Kingdom. They range in age from thirteen to seventy-eight, with an average age of thirty three. The letters have been edited for reasons of space, but I have retained their original language and syntax as often as possible. In exchange for the use of these letters, I have promised anonymity to their writers. All of the names that appear in this book are pseudonyms.

Introduction

I will tell you about a girl.

Eighteen years old, and she was on a quest. Late at night in her university's main library, she searched up and down the stacks. In the psychology aisles, the women's studies aisles, the sociology aisles, night after night. What was the title of the book she sought? She did not know. She knew only that it would be a book about girls without mothers and that it would help her understand herself. It would help explain why, more than a year after her mother had died of breast cancer, she couldn't talk about her mother or even hear her name without starting to weep.

Each night that winter she stepped back out of the library into the inky, freezing wind, wrapped her scarf around her face, and walked back to her dorm room. She was no more informed than she'd been that afternoon. But she'd made it through another day without a mother. That was something.

Some days were harder than others. Like Sundays, when the other girls lay on their beds, talking on their telephones to mothers back at home. And one particular Monday in May, when a group of her friends invited her to join them on a walk downtown to buy Mother's Day cards. The request felt like a knife in her gut. She made up a hasty excuse: she had a prior commitment. It wasn't a lie. She had important things to do. Places to go. A person she needed to become, and quickly, just in case everything was taken away too soon.

But other days were uneventful. Normal, even. She went to class. She joined a sorority. She rode the El train to a part-time job, learned to make pesto, met a boy who used the word "love" and meant it. Some days, she could almost believe she was just like the other girls, the ones with intact families, whose mothers called every Sunday.

The girl finished college, got a job, returned to graduate school. But at every new transition and at every setback, her mother was not there for her to call. Not there to say, *Good job!* or *Don't worry, sweetie. It'll be okay.* Sometimes this made her sadder than she ever thought possible. And sometimes it gave her the motivation she needed to work harder, do better, become that cheerleader and source of comfort for herself.

She never found the book she needed, not even after eight years of searching. So she started writing it herself. Other motherless women clamored to be interviewed. No one had ever asked them to share their stories before. Sure, they had books they could read about grief and mourning, psychology books about early parent loss, and memoirs by sons and daughters who told stories of loss, pain, and recovery. But most of these "grief" texts were about crisis management, not about long-term effects. None of them explained how you should feel four, seven, twelve years later. They didn't explain the impulse to stay connected to a dead mother or that it was all right to still have moments of sadness and hopelessness in between moments of joy.

The girl knew that people in pain hope for a quick fix. She was no exception. When she began writing the book, she hoped it would give her an intense, self-contained period of grief she could eventually exit and finally (finally!) feel that she didn't miss her mother—or having a mother—anymore.

But she soon discovered how unrealistic this was. The daughters she met, some whose mothers had died thirty years in the past, missed their mothers (and, yes, cried for them) still. And so she had no choice but to put this in the book and tell readers the truth: that a daughter's mourning for a mother who died young never completely goes away. A daughter doesn't "get over" the loss, but she eventually does graduate to an emotional state where she holds close the memory of her mother and their time together as an insignia, a talisman, and a guide.

As you've probably realized, the girl in this story is me. Or, to be more accurate, the younger version of myself. When I wrote the first editions of *Motherless Daughters* and *Letters from Motherless Daughters* in the 1990s, I was on a quest to break the silence surrounding early parent loss. At the time we'd all been led to believe that mourning was a linear process and those who didn't ascend to a perpetual state of "acceptance" had somehow failed. Fortunately, over the past twenty years Western culture has become much more aware and more fluent about the ongoing nature of grief. The "stages of grief" made so popular by Elisabeth Kübler-Ross's *On Death and Dying* have been forgone in favor of other models.

Psychologist J. William Worden's "four tasks of mourning" is the one now used by most children's bereavement programs. His four tasks include

1) accepting the reality of the loss,
2) experiencing the pain of the loss,
3) adjusting to an environment without the loved one in it, and
4) finding a new and appropriate place for the lost loved one within the mourner's emotional life.

This fourth task is critically important. As the landmark Harvard Childhood Bereavement Study of the 1990s, of which Worden was a primary author, revealed, children who lose parents don't care about stages of grief. They adapt in ways that feel most natural and necessary to them. Maintaining an emotional connection to a parent who died is just part of what children *do*. As Worden explains in his book *Children and Grief*,

> Through a process we call "constructing" the deceased, the child develops an inner representation of the dead parent that allows him or her to maintain a relationship with the deceased, a relationship that changes as the child matures and the intensity of grief lessens. The child negotiates and renegotiates the meaning of the loss, and in time, relocates the dead person in his or her life and memorializes that person in a way that allows life to move on.

Daughters are enormously creative when finding ways for memories of their mothers to remain vibrant, meaningful, and inspirational in their current lives. When I was writing *Motherless Daughters* in the early 1990s, and revising it for a second edition in the mid-2000s and again this past year, I was repeatedly struck by how many daughters who could easily have been felled by early tragedy instead came to see adversity as a springboard for inner growth. A relatively new field in psychology called "posttraumatic growth"—which was being developed when I was first writing *Motherless Daughters*—maintains that, in our struggles to create meaning out of tragedy, positive changes often arise. It's an oversimplification to say that whatever doesn't kill us makes us stronger, but it may be true that tragedies that don't crush our spirit can teach us a lot about gratitude, resilience, and survival. These are the badges of a warrior who has passed through fire and emerged transformed.

Losing my mother when I was seventeen was a terrible, confusing, and devastating experience, yes. But it also made me more resourceful, more ambitious, more empathetic, and more grateful than I might have otherwise become. I'm a devoted, hands-on mother because I know now how much a mother matters to a child. I know what a real crisis is, and, believe me, it's not a bad haircut or a crushed fender. And passing the age of forty-two, the age my mother was when she died, truly helped me understand how precious life is. Every day after turning forty-two has felt like a gift. I'm deeply grateful for them all.

Am I the same person I would have been if my mother had lived? Probably not. As motherless daughters, we are who we are because of what our mothers gave us and also because they left too soon. No matter how hard we try, we can't go back to that state we occupied before. The novelist and columnist Anna Quindlen, who was nineteen when she lost her mother to cancer, describes the death as "the dividing line between the self I am and the self I became." Thirty-four-year-old Caitlin, who also was nineteen when her mother died, describes an even more dramatic watershed: "I feel that my life is kind of divided into 'Mom' and 'post-Mom' sections," she explains. "The change started with her illness, but on the day of her death life shifted for me."

But does this have to be a bad thing? Psychologists sometimes use the image of a shattered vase to make this point. Think of one's early life as resembling a beautiful, smooth vase. Then something happens—like the early death of a mother—to shatter that flawless image into shards. Trying to fit the pieces back together into their original state won't work. Even the best glue job will have hairline cracks. But if we think of reassembling those pieces into a different configuration, we can accept that something new and unique can emerge.

One of our biggest challenges as adult daughters without mothers is to see our losses as points of departure rather than as a set of lead weights. In this book, you will read the words of fifty-four motherless women who, over the years, have discovered how to reframe their losses as catalysts for change. You will also read the stories of women still struggling to accept and understand their altered situations. In their own words, they describe their mourning processes and the lingering effects of early mother loss in their lives: how it continues to replay itself through later losses; inspires a fear of subsequent loss; leads to idealization of a less-than-perfect mother; affects long-term relationships with fathers, siblings, and other relatives; influences decisions about job, home, and friends; and impacts a woman's roles as a partner, wife, and mother.

Mourning is a highly individual process, its characteristics and intensity determined by a daughter's age when her mother died, the cause of her loss, the quality of the mother-daughter relationship, and the support system available both at the time of loss and in subsequent years. Instead of offering a step-by-step process for resolving one's grief, this book is meant to illustrate the varied experiences motherless daughters have and to shed some light on how the mourning process of a motherless daughter changes over time.

The motherless women whose letters appear in this book clearly constitute a sisterhood. The details of loss and adaptation vary greatly, yet common threads weave in and out of their stories. Reading them, I can hear my younger self speaking in the words of the teen-aged girls; locate myself in the letters from adult women who've come further in understanding and integrating their early losses; and, from the stories of much older women, imagine how I might still be renegotiating my relationship with my mother ten years from now. Their stories all reveal how daughters can move forward without leaving their mothers behind.

It's true that some of the letters detail the intense pain and struggles that girls experience after losing their mothers and that some writers have achieved a deeper degree of healing and insight than others. But it's also true that each daughter in the book is on her own personal path from a place of vulnerability and deprivation to a place of reflection and acceptance. The youngest girls have just begun their journeys and are uncertain of the future twists and turns. The most senior women can reflect on how early mother loss influences the rest of a daughter's life. All of their letters tell stories of courage and hope and determination, stories that can stand as inspirations to us all.

Letters from Motherless Daughters

CHAPTER ONE

Adjustment and Acceptance: The First Year

At a public lecture I once gave about early mother loss, an audience member in the back of the room (we'll call her Allison) raised her hand. "Unlike most of you in this room, I just lost my mother four months ago," she explained, struggling to keep her voice steady. "I'm not yet at a point where I can even talk about it much. What I really want to know tonight is, When am I going to start feeling better? When does the pain finally go away?"

Another woman (we'll call her Rosa) stood up and told the group, "I think the fact that we're all here tonight is proof that the hurt never stops. But I also think the fact that we're here tonight proves that you can get through this and that even though the pain never goes away, you eventually *can* get on with your life." She turned toward Allison. "Let us be examples for you of women who've suffered this loss and survived."

Although Allison and Rosa have lived through similar losses, today they're viewing motherlessness from opposite ends of a continuum. Rosa, whose mother died twenty years ago, has accumulated years of experience with mourning, giving her the authority to act as a guide and a reference point for the newly motherless daughter. But Allison, only four months past the loss, is still in what psychologists call the "acute grief" phase, which begins upon the death of a loved one and ends only as we accept and start integrating the loss into our daily lives.

This acute, or crisis, phase is often characterized by several of the following responses: heightened anxiety; anger; depression; helplessness; irritability; restlessness; pining; persistent wishes to reverse the loss; obsessive thoughts of reunion; bargaining (with the lost loved one or with God); a preoccupation with self-blame (characterized by "I should have . . . " or "if only I'd . . . "); decreased energy and motivation; sleep disturbances; vivid dreams of the deceased; feeling watched by the loved one; keeping the loved one's personal objects close by; weight loss or gain; fear of madness; a tendency to rely on cigarettes, drugs, or alcohol more than usual; and physical problems such as chest pains, stomach pains, frequent headaches, or otherwise inexplicable symptoms. For many daughters, especially those who lost loved ones suddenly and unexpectedly, the acute grief phase may be filled with shock, numbness, and blame. In adults, this crisis period usually lasts for about six to eight months. That's one reason many of us were told that we should be "over" a loss within six months, as if grief could be contained within such a rigidly prescribed period of time. Anyone who has suffered a significant loss as an adult knows that after six or eight months the initial daze does start to dissolve, but that hardly means the mourner's tasks are complete. Instead, the daughter who emerges from the crisis period finds she now has to get down to the very difficult job of confronting the painful reality of her loss.

For children and adolescents, the first six or eight months after a mother's death or departure may feel more like a period of disorganization and household chaos than like a phase of acute emotional distress. After six months, grieving may not even have begun. That's because many children won't grieve until their surviving caretaker has passed through his or her critical emotional period and appears able to attend to other family members' emotional needs.

Even then, a young daughter's capacity to mourn for her mother is directly related to two factors: the response of her surviving parent or primary caregiver and the availability of a supportive environment in which she feels safe to express her sadness, anger, blame, or guilt. Ideally, that support system includes a surviving parent, siblings, family friends, and peers, but even one stable adult with a demonstrated interest in that child's well-being can help a daughter grieve. As J. William Worden explains in *Children and Grief,*

> Constructing a connection to the deceased is a process that involves family members talking about the loss. Highly connected children tended to come from families that were rated closer and more cohesive. These families experienced lower levels of stress and there was an emphasis on religious and spiritual support. In such families both the surviving parent and the child were willing to talk about, to memorialize, and to relocate the lost member as part of the family process.

But not all families are able to grieve openly or together. This is why bereavement groups for children and teens, led by a trained adult, can have such beneficial and long-lasting effects.

Daughters without such an adult to depend on may suppress or deny their true feelings for years, stuffing them under layers of stoicism and false maturity. It's not unheard of for a daughter to experience her first grief response ten or twenty years after her mother's death, when she finally feels independent and stable enough to succumb to the intense emotions she's been suppressing throughout the intervening years.

As the letters from girls and women who've lost their mothers within the past year illustrate, most teens do experience some evidence of acute grief. Seventeen-year-old Kirsten writes of her shock and numbness; thirteen-year-old Jennifer describes her depression and difficulty keeping up in school. Adult daughters write about nighttime anxiety attacks and persistent feelings of deep emptiness and loneliness.

The women in this chapter speak of wrestling with disbelief and the inability to wrap their minds around the simple fact that someone who was here every day of their lives could abruptly be so *not here* when she's still needed so much. They write about the surreal experience of seeing business as usual continue around them when it feels as if everything in their private world has changed. The first weeks, and even months, may feel like moving through a fog, like going through the motions of a funeral and its aftermath on an emotional autopilot. As psychologist Phyllis Silverman explains in *Never Too Young to Know*, "It is almost as if the body has a way of protecting mourners from the full impact of the death," which would otherwise be too overwhelming to bear.

The first full year after the loss of a mother requires a significant individual and family adjustment. No longer is Mom home to care for the younger siblings, offer support to her children, organize holiday celebrations, or keep Dad company.

That initial twelve-month cycle is also important because it allows a family to experience a series of "firsts"—first Thanksgiving without Mom, first Christmas, first Mother's Day, first anniversary of her death—as an altered unit. When fathers begin dating seriously or remarry during this period, daughters often feel angry and resentful about having to accommodate a new family member so quickly or about feeling that they now have to experience each "first" alone.

As all these daughters quickly learned, early loss is a maturing experience. Even the youngest writers have begun to think more expansively than many others their age, describing a need to help other family members and a desire to find inner strength. Sixteen-year-old Erika writes about having an awareness of her own mortality, and Courtney, seventeen, eloquently describes her personal definition of "peace."

Whatever the specific circumstances, the first twelve months or so after a mother's death are typically a chaotic, stressful, and contemplative time, as the following letters reveal.

* * *

Jasmine,

twenty-two, whose mother died of breast cancer two weeks ago

My mother passed away on the first of this month. Her funeral was the Monday just gone. I am the youngest of three girls in the family and am in my fourth year of studies. My mother so desperately wanted to see me get my degree, and it breaks my heart that she won't be at my graduation. I have just started to go back to university after two weeks off and in all honesty am not ready, but I don't feel I have a choice.

My mum is gone and the world hasn't stopped. My studies are still there, and my exams and dissertation won't go away and allow me to curl up in bed for a few months like I want to.

I'm struggling and terrified for the future. I think the most difficult thing is my dad has taken it the hardest. To make matters worse, I have a very poor relationship with my dad. I often communicated with him via my mother. Conversations with him make me anxious. My mum was my whole world, and now my whole world has collapsed around me.

Anyway, I hope that I can come out of this struggle somehow and maybe be able to update you with progress in the future. I just needed to share with someone (outside my family) who truly understands what I'm going through.

Kirsten,

seventeen, whose mother died of cancer four months ago

My mother died when I was seventeen, which seems ridiculous to say, because I am still seventeen. She died a scant four months ago. To be honest with you, it all seems so unreal. I can feel my heart ticking like a time bomb, and I know that sooner or later I will explode and everything that I am not feeling today will come hurtling to the surface.

I want to know if what I am feeling is normal. There is no one that I can talk to about this. After a little while, people don't think I have a problem; they assume that I've "gotten over it," when in all actuality I have not even grasped the fact that this is real. I have not yet lived long enough without my mother to realize what I am missing. I still expect to find her around every corner. I don't know if this is a normal reaction or if I'm just going crazy. Therapy is not an option, for I have no money.

Thank you for writing your book for people like me.

Erika,

sixteen, whose mother died during surgery four and a half months ago

At the beginning of this past summer, I flew three thousand miles away to work in my uncle's coffeehouse. I went because things hadn't been going well between me and my parents during the past two years, and I told them in the spring that I wanted to get away from them for the summer. It was decided that I would spend the summer working for my uncle.

Two months earlier, my mother had told my older brother and me that she had fibroid tumors in her uterus and a few ovarian cysts. Her gynecologist told her that she would have to have a hysterectomy—not as soon as possible but within the next few months.

I worked for my uncle for about two and a half weeks before I realized I just didn't want to be out there anymore. I couldn't think of a good reason why, but I just wanted to go back home so badly. I called my parents at 1:00 in the morning and asked them if I could come home. I had really missed them a lot, and realized I had left for the wrong reasons. When I talked to my mother, she was all groggy, but she was happy to hear that I wanted to come home. I made a reservation with the airline to go home the following Monday. Then I went to bed.

The next morning I talked to my father, and he seemed to have changed his mind. He told me to just give it another week. My mother agreed to this, too. So I called the airline and changed my flight. I kept that reservation, and when I landed at the airport, there was my mother, smiling, waiting for me at the gate. She held her arms out to me, and I hugged her for the last time. Then my father said we had to go to the baggage claim.

The next morning at 9:00 my mother was scheduled to have surgery, not to have an actual hysterectomy but to just have the fibroids and cysts removed. I slept late that morning, till about 11:00. That afternoon was a hazy, balmy one, and I wandered around feeling shitty about myself because I had no idea how I was going to spend the rest of the summer. I went home around 2:30. When I got home, there wasn't much to do but unpack. I sat in front of the TV in the living room unpacking. It was raining outside, and I felt so crappy.

Around 4:45 or so, my brother and my father came home. They came into the living room looking very serious. My brother turned off the TV and sat down on the chair at the other side of the room. My father sat down next to me on the couch and took my hands. He said to me, "She's gone. We lost her."

I immediately burst into tears.

It turns out that the surgery itself had gone okay, but while the doctor was sewing her back up, her blood pressure dropped and she lost her vital signs. The heart team worked on her for more than an hour trying to resuscitate her. Nothing.

It didn't take long to spread the word. By Friday of that week, enough people knew so that more than 250 showed up for her memorial service. Two of my mother's best friends and her boss gave eulogies.

Before the service I saw her lying in that casket and just got so angry. My mother, in all her beauty, in all her greatness, in all her wit, wisdom, skill, and integrity, had been reduced to a pile of flesh. I cried hysterically and my brother held me as he bawled, too.

Death is the most undignified thing there is. God is mean for doing it to us. My wonderful, hardworking mother was now dead. All through the service I begged God to please take her and make her alive again, somehow. If it was to be in heaven, fine. Anywhere, just as long as she represented more than that pile of flesh.

That was a little over four months ago. I was still fifteen then. My mother was forty-nine. We still don't know exactly what went wrong, but we don't really care yet. The fact that she's dead is enough to try to swallow, never mind how it happened.

I started my junior year of high school this September and went on with my life, minus my mother. I see the same therapist I've been seeing since last spring. I'm very close with my guidance counselor, too. I take acting classes, and I'm trying as hard as I can to do well in school. My friends and neighbors have been very nice to me.

My brother has his own apartment about an hour away. He'll be twenty-one this month. I see him once every two weeks or so.

Our house is messy and quiet. But I'm not afraid to be here. I can't be. So many things in my life seem broken up and chaotic, everything except my will to be successful, my inner strength, and my hope. I want to be a great actress someday. That's my dream, and the more I am bombarded with the reminder of mortality, the more I think my dream will come true.

Jennifer,

thirteen, whose mother died of cancer seven months ago

I'm thirteen years old and I'm in junior high. Recently, four parents of kids in my school have passed away. Two of these deaths were caused by cancer. One of these was my mom. She died in December of last year. Now I live with my aunt, and I try to be as considerate as possible. When my mother died, I didn't know what to do. My grades went down, I was depressed all the time, and I just felt like everything was going wrong. I got help from many people—counselors, teachers, people at my church. Nothing seemed to help. But with God's help I have managed to go on with my life. I have to, for my little brother and my little sister. Now I'm much better, but it still worries me.

Many teenagers take their mothers for granted. I want them to understand they shouldn't. When my mom was getting more and more ill, I told her as many times as I could that I loved her and that she was the best. It's very hard for a person like me to say nice things, but she was my mother and she was dying. I hope that other teens don't have to go through all that to be able to say "I love you" to a parent. Because you can't turn time back.

Lori,

fifteen, whose mother died of leukemia seven months ago

My mother was diagnosed with leukemia after a month-long bout with gingivitis. I learned that she had cancer while driving home with my two brothers and my father from my bat mitzvah rehearsal dinner. My mother was transferred to the hospital where my father works. I cried almost every night, terrified of what was happening to my mother and what the consequences would be. My mother was not even able to attend my bat mitzvah because the doctors did not want her to catch any unnecessary germs.

My mother came home for a month to prepare herself for a bone marrow transplant, which occurred at a hospital six hundred miles away. I saw my mom twice in the next three months. In that time period, her hair completely fell out and was replaced by a wig. During the time when my mother was away, I was suddenly burdened with responsibilities that I had taken for granted when my mother was healthy: feeding the dog, making my lunch, changing my sheets, making dinner, watching my brothers. Four months later, my mother's health suddenly declined. She had suffered through the bone marrow transplant, countless doses of chemotherapy, and much more. I was over at a friend's house when their telephone rang. It was a close family friend calling to tell me that my mother had lapsed into a coma. I remember the whole world going black as I kneeled down on my friend's kitchen floor, sobbing with the knowledge that my mother was going to die.

That night was the worst night of my life. I hardly slept the entire night, but paced the hallways with anxiety. I prayed to God to save my mother, to not let her die. My brothers and I were so young . . . we needed her. Twenty-four hours after she had fallen into a coma, my mother woke up. Her recovery from it was rapid, and within a few days she could sit up and talk. She continued to come home for short periods of time, almost every weekend, until one week she went back into the hospital and stayed there. Nine months after her diagnosis, my mother died in the hospital. My brothers were six and twelve, and I was fourteen.

Although I went to school the day after she died, I wasn't prepared for the sympathetic looks and somber whisperings of my classmates. I went home early. I went to the funeral service for my mother, but I didn't go to the cemetery. I wasn't prepared to see my mother, my once energetic, loving, beautiful mother placed into a box and lowered into the ground.

Both my brothers and I have recently started to go to counseling. I find it very helpful, as well as writing in my diary. As a result of my mother's death, my family has become closer. I now confide in my father. Before my mother's death, I only saw him from 6:30 p.m. until 9:00 p.m. every night. I also realize that I am lucky, despite my mother's death. It sounds funny to say that there has been some good that came out of this tragedy, but there has. I learned a lot during the period of her illness. As my mother told me one day before she went into the hospital for the first time, "You may not always hear me, but you'll always feel my answer."

Darlene,

forty-six, whose mother died of complications from multiple sclerosis seven months ago

After five days in the ICU and a valiant twenty-five-year battle against MS, my mother gestured for me to come closer to her hospital bed and whispered in my ear, "I am tired of fighting." I'm not sure if she made a conscious decision to share this life-altering news with me, her oldest daughter and her full-time caregiver, or if it was merely a matter of happenstance. Either way, those five words signaled a change in course not only in the path of medical treatment but also in the path of my life. With the help of a palliative care doctor, we abandoned the life-sustaining strategy we had in place and switched our focus to keeping Mom comfortable and pain-free in her final hours. With twenty-two members of our family by her side and my father holding her hand and singing the iconic song, "Unforgettable," she took her last breath.

It's been seven months since my mom passed away. In some aspects, coping with grief reminds me of my mom's struggle with MS. There are periods of time where your symptoms diminish, and then, seemingly out of nowhere, you relapse. Still, the illness is always there, just as the pain of losing a loved one stays with you forever. The challenge lies in learning to live with that pain, and unfortunately there's no "one size fits all" solution.

Even within my immediate family, we have different approaches to coping with grief, and this can be a source of tension, particularly between my oldest brother and me. Recently, he sat me down and expressed concern that "Mom has been gone for seven months and you don't seem to be moving on with your life." Understandably, his remark left me feeling injured. It also underscores the following issues: 1) each one of us grieves in our own way and 2) there's no set timetable for processing grief.

I know that my brother's comment stems from a place of love and genuine concern, but his perception that I am not moving past my grief fast enough left me feeling isolated. As it is, I find myself withdrawing from people, even those people who've made multiple attempts to reach out to me. I feel different from the person I was before. At first, I was apologetic about the change in me, but with time I've come to understand that grief changes you and that's okay. Just as other experiences shape who we are, grief has a lasting effect on us, too.

While my brother and I have our respective approaches to grief, I know that he is there for me, and the same is true for my siblings and my father. We are fortunate to have each other and to share such a close-knit relationship. It makes the good times that much sweeter, and it makes the bad times more bearable. I've also found comfort in online and in-person support groups for daughters who've lost their mothers, in books, and in the music of Bruce Springsteen, the man who has provided the soundtrack for all the monumental events in my life, both the joyous and the heartbreaking.

Last year, I entered a writing contest with the prompt "Who Inspires You?" Out of four thousand entries, my essay won the grand prize. I was shocked, but, as I told others, it was less shocking when you consider that my mom was the source of my inspiration. Not a day goes by when I don't think of her or wish that she was still here with us, but I know that the lessons of how she lived will carry me through this dark period and maybe, just maybe, my experience of coping with her death will serve as an example to other daughters who are going through this same tragic experience.

Courtney,

seventeen, whose mother died of bile duct cancer eight months ago

My father passed away ten years ago of a heart attack, when I was seven. My mum was on a holiday when it happened but flew home immediately. I don't think there is ever a right age or time to lose someone, but, with saying that, I was so young when my dad suddenly passed away.

After everything we had been through with my dad dying, I thought nothing bad could ever happen to my family again. But then my mum was diagnosed with cholangiocarcinoma, a rare cancer that affects just 2 in 250,000 people. I watched her go through countless chemotherapy and radiation treatments, hallucinations, and waking up in the ICU.

The next year, when we were told she'd have two months to live, my brave mother decided to stop all treatment and spend what quality time she had left at home with her loved ones. She knew in her heart that, no matter how many more needles they stuck into her, she was terminal and it was her time. Thirteen days later, my amazing mother passed away at our home surrounded by her family and friends whom she loved.

I didn't have as much time with my dad as I'd had with my mum. When my dad passed I wasn't thinking about every detail in the future and how his death would affect the rest of my life. But with Mum it was totally different because I was a teenager. Although I had warning, I knew it was still going to hurt. I was not only grieving the fact that she was going to die but was also dealing with the loss of our future together—having her there on my wedding day and watching her become a grandma. Being told she only had two months left really brought everything into perspective. That's one thing I always think about: that it shouldn't take your mum telling you she has cancer and two months left to live for you to tell her how much you love her, thank her every day for all she has done, and to appreciate everything around you.

I can never predict when I'll experience surges of grief. It'll catch me at the most random of times. For example, I'll be driving and suddenly remember a memory and burst out into tears. I've learned that everyone deals with grief in their own way and that if you fight your feelings, you will only make things worse for yourself. So now when I need to cry I will and when I need time alone, I'll have it. I also remind myself often that it's okay not being strong all the time, that I can break down and that it's normal.

I believe that peace is a really hard concept to define. I think people believe that peace is something that, when you have it, you're suddenly enlightened and you're set for the rest of your life. But in my opinion, peace is a constant struggle. Some days you feel you have it and you feel really great, but on other days you don't and you feel really down. Peace for me means having those moments where you say to yourself, "I'm going to be okay, I'm happy right now and that might change tomorrow and that's okay, but for now I'm happy and I'm going to embrace it."

Two months after my mum passed, I made a decision to move out because I could no longer live with my mum's partner whom she had married five months before she passed. I expressed how I was feeling to two of my close family friends, and the next day I packed my suitcase and handbag and moved in with a family friend. I lived there for six weeks and it was great, but I knew I had to figure out my next move. This ended up being my auntie's house, where I now live. I've never looked back after making that decision and have never been happier. My auntie always lets me know that she is there for me no matter what and would support me in any decision I make. My auntie also gave me all the time in the world to get back up on my own two feet.

I think it's important for others to realize that people heal in their own way and time and that it shouldn't feel forced. I believe that in time you find your own way of dealing with things so you should not get frustrated when you're struggling. Also, at the end of the day no one can heal yourself but you. Advice from others can only go so far; it's you that has to make the decision to keep moving. It's important to remind yourself that you're your own person and you are finding your place in this world. If that means taking all the time in the world, then so be it.

I also believe it's important to recognize that you can't help what has happened to you in the past but you can decide where to go in the future. You are not the mistakes you make. You are what you choose to be today and how you treat the people around you. My auntie really helped me understand this, and I hope it's something that more people become conscious of.

Tina,

twenty-six, whose mother died of cancer one year ago

My beautiful mom, Susan, died last year at the much-too-young age of forty-six. I never got to say a real good-bye to her because the asshole doctors kept telling us she was going to make it until she finally had to be put on a respirator and it was too late. From the time we found out she had a tumor in her lung to the time she died was about three weeks. My dad is now forty-nine (and already engaged!) and I have a ten-year-old sister. (She's adopted, so she's now lost two mothers.)

My mom's death was the most horrible thing that has ever happened to me. Even though I am a constant worrier, I never once considered that she would die. After her death, I had to do things I wouldn't wish on anyone. I had to tell my little sister that our mom was dead—all I remember is her gut-wrenching shriek and when I said our mom's heart gave out, her screaming, "Why couldn't they have given her a pig's heart?" I had to write her obituary. I had to collect her clothes for the funeral home and pick out her coffin and flowers. I had to clean out her closet.

My mom had me when she was only twenty-one. She said we all "grew up together." We were best friends and would talk on the phone almost every day. She always talked about how we would be little old ladies together. She couldn't wait until my husband and I had a baby. She was a genuinely wonderful woman with a wacky sense of humor and the kindest heart. One thousand people came to her funeral.

She used to get up in the middle of the night instinctually when I was sick, hold my hair back when I was throwing up, and get me a glass of Pepsi to get rid of the bad taste. When I was little, she would tell me that she would never let anything bad happen to me. She told me stories about moms who, with adrenaline, would lift cars to save their children and said she would do that for me, too. When my husband and I moved into our first apartment, she came over to scrub out all the cabinets and help me set up the kitchen. When I was reading my poetry at a coffeehouse, she got all dressed up in a black turtleneck and came to hear me—sipping decaf and sitting in a rickety chair, making conversation with all the café types— she was so proud. She was just that kind of mom, and sometimes I can't believe she's never coming back.

When she died, even though I had never been to a therapist before, I knew that this was really bad and I wouldn't be able to make it on my own. I thought I'd go for a few sessions and get it all straightened out, but—ha!—I soon realized I was in a bottomless pit of grief. It's only now, after a year, that the therapist thinks I can take a little break from my weekly visits.

I was in horrible shape. I cried every night until I could barely breathe, and my husband would get up to get me half a Xanax (ever so thoughtfully provided by the hospital when my mom died). Work meant nothing to me. I was really hurt when my dad started dating a woman a month after my mom's funeral and expected me to be happy for him. I felt horrible grief and guilt trying to take care of my little sister as best I could while maintaining my own life—taking her to a sex-ed class at her school when it should have been my mom, buying her underwear when I realized she had outgrown it all, cutting her fingernails, begging her to write thank-you notes so no one would think she didn't have manners, and just making sure she didn't look like a pitiful orphan. I felt like no one understood. People tried to be nice, especially friends of my mother, but everyone eventually goes back to their routine and you still have to deal with the mess.

Like you, I looked for an appropriate book in countless bookstores. I'm that kind of person. When I don't know how to do something, I'll read a book. There was nothing on this. The Kübler-Ross stuff pissed me off. The New Age stuff depressed me. Books about angels comforted me in a small way, but I wanted a guidebook to tell me what to expect—to tell me what to do with a million pairs of my mother's shoes, to tell me what to do with her bras, to tell me what to do when none of the relatives wanted to come over to the house for Christmas because they said it was too depressing.

Your book talks to the loneliest, most private void in my heart. It tells me that I'm not a freak with an abnormal attachment to my mother because I'm still grieving after a year. It tells me that all my feelings and experiences (suddenly not wanting a baby, insisting on wearing my mom's twenty-five-year-old hippie poncho, hating cute older women I see in the market, etc.) are pretty normal, or at least that other people have gone through them.

I will admit that my mom's death had some good points, if you could call them that. I have a new, mature relationship with my father, small things don't stress me out anymore, I am more passionate about everything—I really appreciate a beautiful day, good food, friends, my husband—and I have finally formed a "family unit" with my husband that exists independently of my dad and sister.

I don't want my mom's life to have been in vain. She never went to college, but she was incredibly bright and read voraciously. She wanted so much for me. Even though it never would have come to that, she said she would wait tables to put me through college, and I know she would've. This is one of the things that haunts me: she was really creative and thinking about going to a gemology college to learn to make jewelry but didn't go because she thought $7,000 was too expensive. I later saw the check my dad wrote to the funeral home and mortuary to pay for everything—it was $7,000. Sick irony.

Do I still hurt? Yes, and I always will. There is so much stuff that I want to ask her! I want to dial the house and have her pick up the phone. I want to hear her laugh. I want to hug her. I want to give her a beautiful grandchild to spoil. I want her to smooth my hair the way she did. Oh, I could go on and on. You know the rest. . . . The stories are all the same.

Elaine,
forty, whose mother died of cancer one year ago

I'm an adopted child, and for the past twenty-one years I lived with my adoptive mother. I might add that for the most part we lived as friends. You see, I missed what I felt would have been a very important part of my life. During my teens, my parents divorced, and I was unable to understand that my mother was having as difficult a time as I was. The family was split apart, and there was a great deal of bitterness on both sides. My mother and I butted heads, and I was already more mature than my years in a lot of ways, but perhaps not in the ways that may have really counted and would have helped me to get through the situation that we were all facing.

I moved in with my father when I was thirteen years old. I was an oddity and was thought very strangely of, as my father was a salesman and was out of town a lot. I was left to my own devices. During that time, I didn't realize what a hard time my mother was having. She was struggling to put her life together, had sold her home, and was renting a home and pursuing her artwork. I was really pissed off with her because she didn't come to my high school graduation. It wasn't until I was eighteen and already married that I realized how much I loved her and missed her. She was very ill at that time—I didn't know how ill until afterwards. The rest of the family made it a point to keep me informed but not to emphasize just how serious it really was. Their fear was that I would come home and she would realize she was dying, for there would certainly be no other reason for me to come that far, as I was just married and had really no money to speak of. They thought she would have given up the fight.

She was hospitalized for thirty-three days. During that time the doctors had informed her parents three different times not to go home, that she wasn't going to make it through the night. What a hellacious situation for her parents, and yet their thoughts were to protect both her and me.

Already, my husband and I were having some problems and thought that perhaps one way to resolve them might be to move. I asked my mother if we could come to her home. This was only months after her serious health situation. She had absolutely no reservations and allowed us to come to her home. She never set a time limit as to how long we could stay—her home was our home. The marriage didn't last, and she helped me pick up the pieces. It wasn't long afterward that she was hospitalized again and I realized that I might lose her. I had already felt as though I'd lost her during those years between the ages of thirteen and eighteen. I just wasn't ready for this.

We became so very close just before the surgery. I had always wanted that closeness from her. She wasn't always able to give it, as she hadn't been given it as a child. She had been raised in different homes until about the age of ten.

For the next several years, her health was not the best, but she did very little complaining. I was always the one who was worried about her and would push her to go to the doctor when I was certain she wasn't feeling well. She was there for me when I found a lump in my right breast at the age of twenty-three. She went with me to the doctor, waited for me, talked to the doctor and explained that I was very scared and asked him to prescribe something so that I would at least be able to sleep until the results came back. I had several other surgeries as time went by, including the one where I decided I didn't want to have children. My mother was a woman who was unable to have children and had wanted me and adopted me, yet she stood by the decision I made. She kept my secrets. She was my best friend.

My mother hung in there with me when I had bouts of depression or when some stupid man was in my life and I was allowing him to make me miserable. I was always an overweight child, and she never allowed anyone to call me fat. I finally decided to go through Weight Watchers and lost a substantial amount of weight. It took me two years to do it, but she was there all the way, helping me keep up the fight.

When I was twenty-one, she encouraged me to seek out my biological mother and gave me every bit of information that she could recall. After I received a letter from my biological mother, she drove me to the airport, even though she was terrified of driving there, with all the traffic and her fear of getting lost. We cried and said good-bye—she, fearful that I wouldn't come back; me, fearful that she wouldn't want me to, as though I had betrayed her in some way. I was never so glad to get home as I was after that trip to visit my biological mother, Beverly. I swore then that although Beverly had given birth to me, the woman I called "Mom" and would always call "Mom" had given me life.

My mother left me two days before her seventy-first birthday and two weeks before my fortieth. When we knew that she wasn't going to have much longer, she asked me to take her home. The hardest thing that I have ever done was to bring my mother home to let her die.

I have never felt as lonely as I have these past months without her. My best friend is gone. I know that the grieving and this emptiness I feel, this gaping hole in the pit of my soul, is not something that is going away easily. Although it will perhaps take a lifetime to get over this loss, I am learning to celebrate the joy in all the things that she left me. I know that she left me her green thumb, and the house that we shared for so long I've made my own, which I know she would have wanted. I still hear her voice, calling to me to come see a beautiful sunset that she was observing while painting a Christmas card for someone special. It's almost that time of year now, and I will miss the smell of the cookies that she always baked. She loved this time of year so. She would start to decorate the house around Thanksgiving and would insist that I get her a tree for Christmas.

The last year of my mother's life was a strange one for me, at best. I started to experience a lot of stress, which caused me a great deal of pain in the chest area. I was frantic, which just seemed to exacerbate the problem. This started about two years ago and continued until about two months ago. The doctor I was seeing for this problem sent me to a psychologist. At the time, I had no idea that my mother had lung cancer. It didn't become evident to me until two weeks before she died. She had managed to keep it a secret for that long. My doctor's nurse thinks that perhaps somehow I knew about my mother's condition, because there didn't seem to be a medical reason for my chest pains.

I still see a therapist at this point, and I'm trying very hard to put things together in my life. I know that I was very fortunate to have had my mother. She was no saint, and certainly neither am I. I am just very lucky to have had a best friend like her. The real point of all this is to say it doesn't really matter how old you are. The loss of a mother hurts—hurts terribly. It doesn't matter the age.

CHAPTER TWO

Searching for Meaning: One to Five Years

As daughters slowly move beyond the searching that's so common to the initial grief process, repeated failures to reunite with their lost mothers help them begin to realize and accept that their mothers are truly gone. After the first year they have passed through the "year of firsts"—first holiday season without Mom, first birthday without Mom, first anniversary of her death. Although these dates may be painful reminders of her absence, the daughter who is more than one year postloss has no choice but to acknowledge that all other aspects of life continue, with or without Mom.

She may still feel some disbelief, but its quality has begun to change. No longer does a daughter have trouble believing the mother is gone; she now finds herself having trouble believing that so much is happening in her absence and that so much has passed. Her impulse to pick up the telephone and call her mother has transformed into the wish that her mother was there to call.

Twenty-one-year-old Sherri, whose mother died after sur-gery four years ago, describes how her grief has evolved since then:

> For the entire year after [my mother's] death, maybe even longer, she was all I could think about. Whenever I made a new acquaintance, I had the urge to blurt out, "My mother is dead," as if I were hiding something from them by not providing that information. When I went into drugstores, cards "For that Special Mother" attacked me as I walked down the aisle. I spent many afternoons and nights—too many—locked in my dorm room, cry-ing into my teddy bear as I stared with disbelief and de-spair at my favorite picture of our family.
>
> It's nearly impossible to believe that I'm a senior in college and that it's been four years since my mother's death. The pain has never subsided completely—it never will—but I no longer wear it on my sleeve.

As the psychiatrist Vamik Volken explains in *Life After Loss*, a daughter moves into the second stage of mourning as she accepts her loss. Then she begins what he calls "the subtle and complex negotiations" required for her to integrate the memory of her mother into a motherless life. This process often involves an attempt to make sense of the loss and to fit it into her life story in a meaningful way. Most daughters whose losses occurred one to five years ago, like twenty-one-year-old Sherri and twenty-six-year-old Jean, find they're still searching for that meaning. The platitudes and clichés—such as "God must have needed another angel"—that may have sustained a daughter at first feel less satisfying now. She wants weightier explanations for her pain.

At the same time, a motherless daughter in this stage begins to realize how much around her has been permanently altered. The hypothetical "I wonder what life will be like without my mother?" is replaced by "So *this* is what life is like without her." Her family has changed. Her expectations for the future have changed. And as a result, she feels *herself* starting to change.

By this point, even the youngest girls already can see that mourning will not end quickly—and perhaps will not end at all. At one year postloss, fear for a surviving parent's safety may increase. Anxiety about one's own safety may also start to rise. The Harvard Child Bereavement Study found that children's self-esteem levels decline between one and two years after a parent's death. But the study also found at the one-year point that three-quarters of the children who'd lost a parent felt more "grown up" than their nonbereaved peers. This was especially true for teens and for boys.

Other daughters become determined to find a way to learn from a loss and to apply these lessons as they move forward. Twenty-nine-year-old Ellen wants to become more self-reliant and trust her own intuition. Twenty-one-year-old Sherri is trying to assess what is most meaningful about life and is looking for a way to integrate this philosophy with her long-term plans. Their next steps will be to work toward achieving these new goals and to establish themselves as independent women, without feeling as if they've left their mothers behind.

Quite a few of the women who wrote to me from this point in their mourning spoke of believing their mothers were watching over them and of feeling her presence every day. Seventeen-year-old Kelsey describes her mother, who died one year ago, as her family's "guardian angel." Locating the mother both externally (for example, in heaven) and internally ("she's inside me, always cheering me on") has become important to the daughters in this chapter.

Across the board, daughters who had positive relationships with other surviving family members tended to feel more stable and secure after the first year, and those whose family relationships were strained after the mother's death felt more adrift. This drives home the importance of strong, close family bonds throughout a daughter's grieving process, especially to younger daughters.

* * *

Kelsey,

*seventeen, whose mother died from a suspected seizure thirteen
months ago*

I lost my Mom so suddenly no one in my family saw it coming. She was literally there one day and gone the next. She
wasn't sick; she didn't die of cancer. She had epilepsy—a history of seizures—and we think she had a grand mal seizure
and it killed her.

The year was very trying for all of us, and we're all still adjusting to life without a mother. I've done a lot of growing up
this past year, and, man, do I feel old! For the first few weeks
my dad and I would ask each other, "Can we wake up from
this nightmare yet?" Because that's what it felt like—and still
does at times—that we're living our worst nightmares.

When the coroner took my mom's body outside, my dad
confessed to me, "I never thought I'd outlive your mother." I
was honest and told him, "Neither did I." He wasn't upset by
it. He's a smoker and not in the best of health. Plus he said
that women usually outlive men.

That day was a blur as were the first week and first couple
of months. She was buried exactly a week after her death. We
held services for her Saturday and Sunday because she had
friends and family in two different places. She was buried in
the same cemetery where my grandfather, aunt, and brother
are buried. Now my whole family (dad, sister, brother, and I)
has plots there because, as my mom's death taught us, it's best
to be prepared.

On the anniversary of her death this year, I had to go to school even though I wanted to stay home and mourn/ remember her in my own way. My godmom was probably right, though, when she said that my mom would have preferred me in school rather than moping about at home. At least there were distractions at school.

And here we are, thirteen months after her death, all pretty much the same as we were a year ago. As my best friend Wendy said, "Damn, girl. It feels like your mom was just here with us last week." And it does. The only thing that says a year and a month have gone by are calendars. It still feels unreal.

I read somewhere that the deceased communicate with us in our dreams. And I believe that. Sometimes I can still feel her presence around me. When odd things happen that no one can explain, we say, "Oh, Mom's here," or "Mom did it." She's our guardian angel. My guardian angel. She is watching over me and my family until it is our turn to join her. For now, she's got my grandfather, my brother Matt, and my aunt to keep her company. Personally I'm hoping that my father doesn't join her until he's a grandfather. All my life I expected my mom to help me raise my kids and teach me how to be a good mom, because she was such an excellent one. But now I'll have to look to my dad for that help. Even though he may not be a good mom, he can still teach me how to be a good *parent*. I don't think I'll be able to handle being a new parent without parents of my own for advice.

I honestly don't think I could have survived this past year if it weren't for the help and support of my friends and family. We're not nearly done with the pain just because a year has passed. The pain we will probably just learn to live with. In the meantime, every day this past year was not a struggle to get out of bed. I had and have things to live for. My life was not over just because I lost my Mom. I'm sure by going to school every day and continuing my education I'm making my Mom proud. She'll be with me, forever and always.

Paige,

twenty-two, whose mother died of cancer one year ago

I lost my mother last year to a rare form of cancer. She was only sixty-one. Her death was and still is difficult for me to comprehend because she was really the only person I had who gave me true emotional/mental support. My father is of course an important figure in my life, but he never gave me the same emotional comfort.

My mother and I would talk and do everything together. My life revolved around her. As a housewife, she was always home taking care of the family while my father worked. I never really became independent because she was the "perfect" housewife, able to take care of everything herself. (My mother was Asian so the definition of "housewife" is probably different from American terms.) She never asked for help. I never took the initiative to learn her skills because I had the false sense of security that she would always be with me. But I feel that our dependence on her was one factor that led to her early death.

Everything has changed since she died. I don't know how to run the house, and everyone else is too busy with their lives to take care of us. My brother and father rely on me, and my self-esteem has gotten worse now that my father expects me to take on my mother's role . . . which I don't know how to do. I feel that I demand more attention from others than ever before. I still excel in my schoolwork, but I don't know if it's worth it because my father tells me I fail in housework.

I feel that my role as a daughter is now determined by my mother's housekeeping abilities and by taking on my mother's role. It seems it's okay for my brother and father to be imperfect at housework, but not me. I am supposed to be the strong and understanding one even though I'm the youngest. I want to lean on my father for support, but he gets angry at me and expects me to be his emotional support. And it has affected my relationship with my boyfriend, who I respect a lot, for him to have to take on the understanding, nurturing role in our relationship, even though we are about the same age.

I didn't mean to write such a long letter but I just really wanted a place to write down my thoughts. Thank you very much for this beautiful book. I was able to grieve and not avoid the feelings that come with the loss of my mother.

Monica,

thirty-three, whose mother died of multiple system organ failure after
chemotherapy for leukemia one year ago

Just five days before my daughter was due, my mother was transferred to the ICU with sepsis and bilateral pneumonia requiring intubation. I crumbled the first time I saw her in the hospital. My prayers quickly went from "Please dear God, grant my mom a cure" to "Please dear God, don't take her this week. Not the week the baby is due to enter this world."

Well, she held on. Six days later, the day after my due date, mom's blood cultures weren't growing any bugs (a very good sign), and her respirator was working less, which meant she was breathing more on her own. I could say this was God's little light shining in to give me some strength to deliver my daughter. My labor was induced the next day.

I'd thought it would be easier once the baby was born, but it was not. It was much harder. The next three weeks went by so very, very slowly. Back and forth I went to the ICU. Thank goodness for my loving, supportive husband and my in-laws, who helped with our two-and-a-half-year-old son and the new baby at home.

Mom did not improve. She was too delicate for the powerful chemo. On a beautiful, blue-sky June day, I stood by her ICU bed, rubbing what hair was left on her head, which was her favorite thing next to a back scratch. I whispered in her ear that it was okay, we would be all right, and she could go. Her heart stopped twenty minutes later.

My strong and vibrant mother, only fifty-eight years old, so ecstatic in anticipation of her granddaughter. Just nine weeks earlier, she hadn't been sick at all.

So many people wonder how I did it, how I dealt with the tremendous loss of my mother and bringing my daughter into the world at the same time. I don't have an answer. I know that faith carries me through, still. I have young children and a family to take care of. My mom would not be happy with me if I could not function and be productive, I do know that much. So I go on for her and for my family. It's not better, just a little easier.

I am thankful for so many things: thankful for thirty-three years with my mother and thankful this devastating loss didn't happen twenty-five years ago to leave my father with four children under the age of ten. I'm thankful my mother helped plan my wedding, thankful for her being with me through teenage heartbreaks, proms, and disappointments, and thankful for placing my son in her arms. The smile on her face in pictures where she's holding him lights up the room still.

The weeks that she was ill were unbearable and long. After she passed, the days turned into weeks, then months, and pretty soon here I sit in disbelief I haven't seen my mom or heard her voice in more than a year. Every now and then I see a face that causes me to look twice, a resemblance that sends a chill up my spine. I still dream of her often, so vividly sometimes that I wake up almost disappointed. I choose to believe she is with me always, not missing out, just with a better view.

Alexis,

thirteen, whose mother died suddenly two years ago

My mother died when I was eleven years old. I walked into the living room and found her lying on the couch. Her death was a complete shock to me. She had seemed healthy before.

My mother and I used to fight a lot, and I would say, "I hate you." I know that hurt her so much. I never meant it. I hope she knows that.

The hardest part about my mother's death was going back to school. Kids in my fifth grade class brought me presents, like stuffed animals. I accepted them but wondered why. My entire class made me cards. Even my teacher gave us no work so I wouldn't have any.

The one difference between your family and mine was that mine grew closer and became more dependent on each other. My brother and I started to have long talks. They really helped me. My dad had to work a lot, so my brother and I became loners, in a way.

There are constant reminders of my mother wherever I go. She *still* gets mail and phone calls, and people at my school are always saying, "Let your mom sign this." I know I will never get over her, but I have to get on with my life.

Lynn,

eighteen, whose mother died in a car accident a year and a half ago

My mother died suddenly when I was sixteen. After her death, my family completely changed. We got much closer, but her loss was a real blow to me because life was great until the day she was killed. Everything I see or do reminds me of something she said or did or even the way she spoke with an accent, even today, a year and a half later.

After her death, I was forced to become an independent adult, and I started spinning aimlessly. I found it hard to live the way I was used to. I spent all of my time with friends so I wouldn't let myself have time to think. Unfortunately, I also didn't give myself time to eat. I slowly developed anorexia nervosa, even though I didn't realize what was happening to me. It was only a month ago that I started recovering from it.

I guess I felt that my mother always wanted me to be perfect, so I would become perfect for her after her death as a gift. I didn't realize how thin I was, even when I dropped from a size 12 to a size 8. My friends were worried about me when I didn't eat lunch at school, but I would always just tell them that I liked to eat when I got home—but I never did.

I just wish I could be like any other normal person. Sometimes I feel like I'm going crazy, but I talk to my sister (who's also my best friend), and she usually comforts me. I try to remember that motherless doesn't mean parentless. I still have my father, even though he always worked when I was growing up, so I never even knew him before my mother died. I'm hoping that in the future I will get on with my life and live for the future, not in the past.

Jean,

twenty-six, whose mother died of cancer two years ago

My mother died when I was twenty-four. I'm an only child and have always been extremely independent; now I find that I have more of a sense of separation anxiety than I've ever felt before. It's rather unnerving to be twenty-six and suddenly feeling a shaky foundation where I've never felt one before.

It has greatly affected my romantic relationships in that I have never wanted to feel "tied down" or "stuck" with one man. Now, I'm terrified to be alone, terrified to lose my boyfriend of two and a half years. Yet at the same time I know that the harder I try to hold onto him, the more I'm hurting our relationship. I'm afraid of being left alone by another person I love so dearly, especially if I can "control" this—our relationship. See, I couldn't control her cancer.

I constantly tell myself that there was a reason for her early death . . . and that someday I'll know that answer. I tell myself that "only the good die young" (she was forty-eight). Or I push it all out of my mind when I'm feeling too emotionally drained to deal with it on some days. The knowledge that she will not be picking up the phone when I'm calling my father or dropping what she's doing so that she can talk with me is often heartbreaking. I miss being able to call her at work and just say, "Hi! I was thinking of you."

I work for a family, and I'm privy to a lot of personal confrontations among my employers and their children. When I witness one of the arguments between the eldest daughter and her mother, my heart just breaks. It's not my place to intervene, but my mind's often racing as they're arguing. I want to grab the daughter by the shoulders and say to her, "Hey! It's your *mother* you're yelling at! Why are you wasting such precious time with her by screaming? Enjoy this time—be friends! Because it's all over before you know it."

Pretty crazy, I'm sure. But that's how I feel. I guess it's true to say that, at times, I'm envious of the time and experiences some girls have with their mothers. I would do anything to spend time with mine again, and it hurts me to see people taking for granted *their* time with their loved ones.

It would mean the world to me just to—once again—see my mother smile at me, touch me, and say my name, one last time.

Samantha,

thirty-five, whose mother died of sepsis two years ago

My mom was the woman I strived to be. She was not only my best friend but also the person I idolized and wanted to do everything with. I would often pray to God and tell him I knew there were a lot of wonderful mothers out there but I thanked him for giving me the perfect one for me.

My mom had severe spinal problems that resulted in six neck and back surgeries over a sixteen-year time span. There were days when she would be stuck on the floor in agony, yet she never complained. She never wanted to be a burden to anyone, which eventually led to her decision to do her final spinal surgery.

I grew up constantly aware that my mom's back and neck were very fragile and that one wrong move could be life threatening. I worried about her constantly, and I went to all her surgeries. I would sit in the hospital quietly praying for her to make it through and to feel better. I hated to see her in pain. Thankfully she would always recover and then do way more than she was supposed to, not letting anything hold her back.

Two years ago, the familiar pain came back. By then, she'd had every vertebra in her neck and spine operated on. This time the doctor said she needed a decompression and laminectomy to release the pressure on her spine that was causing immobility in her arms and loss of feeling in her extremities. *Oh no*, I thought. How much could one spine take? But my mom, being the brave mother she was, said she would rather be able to button a blouse and cut her meat than be a burden to her family.

The surgery date was set, and my mind weighed heavy with the stress of losing her on the operating table. She reassured me by saying, "I'm not planning on going anywhere," and I would reply as a joke, "If you see the light, turn away!"

After the surgery, I thought, *We've made it through another one.* But I realized immediately that something wasn't right. This surgery didn't seem to have been as "easy and painless" as the doctor had described it. My mom was in horrible pain and developed an unusual swelling in her face. We later learned this was an early sign of infection. She had to stay in the hospital a few days longer than she wanted. I had been worried about her making it through surgery, but she was more worried about getting a hospital-acquired disease, so she wanted to get out of the hospital as soon as possible.

When she did come home, I got to spend quality time with her, laugh with her, and cook for her. God allowed each one of her four children and many grandchildren to spend one last special day alone with her, not realizing it would be their last. Three weeks after the surgery, my mom was rushed back to the same hospital. She had developed sepsis, a blood infection from the surgery, and the doctors didn't catch it in time. There was no time to say good-bye or "I love you." Within twenty-four hours her whole body was shutting down.

We had just left the hospital to grab a few hours of sleep when the call came to tell us the doctors were trying to revive my mom after she went into cardiac arrest. By the time I got there, she was in a coma. I knew she had waited for me to get there so that I could hold her hand one more time and let her know I was there. A few hours later she went back into cardiac arrest. This time they were not able to revive her.

I often wonder, Is it better to know your loved one is going to die so you can make arrangements and say goodbye or to have her go suddenly without the chance to say "I love you" or good-bye? I choose the latter. After seeing my mom suffer for those miserable twenty-four hours, I know I couldn't have watched her suffer for months or years. The image of her in pain has been burned into my mind forever. I desperately wish I could erase it. My mom didn't want us to see her suffer. She wanted us to remember her as the strong, independent, loving, giving, sparkly person I knew growing up.

The two long years since my mother died have been difficult but life altering. It took me some time to realize that life keeps moving. Her favorite television shows still air, holidays are still celebrated, hard times still come and go, and laughter is still meant to be a part of my life. My husband of nine years has now seen me at my best and worst. I have opened up to him in ways I never would have if my mom were still here. She was my confidant, and when she passed I had to learn to trust others as I'd trusted her. I've realized that I need to let my husband know me in all the ways my mom knew me and trust that he will still love me. From losing my mother, I've learned that life's struggles are meant to be shared and not carried alone. I have learned not to wait until a person is sick or dying to say "I love you" but to say it every day.

I remember my mom with all the beauty and love and compassion that a person can possess. I want to pass on the lessons that she taught me and share the special bond we had with a child of my own one day. I have not yet been blessed with that opportunity, but I know that when it happens there will be a piece of my mom in my newborn's smile.

Ellen,

twenty-nine, whose mother died of hepatitis three years ago

I lost my mom when I was twenty-six. She was an operating-room nurse, and several years before that had been pricked by a needle that was infected with the disease.

As I became an adult, my mom became a child. I was never able to relate to her on a mature, adult level. I was dispensing medication and changing diapers. I was taxi driver, cook, maid—everything but a daughter. I was in college when she was first diagnosed, and until she died I lived and breathed the disease. I didn't date. I didn't go out very much. I gained weight.

When Mom passed away, it was peaceful because she was no longer in pain. I had mourned the loss before she died and thought I was done. I now know I am not. I recently ended a relationship after two and a half years, and I feel abandoned. I should've been way out of it shortly after meeting Allan, but I didn't want to lose another person I loved. He had some problems, so, being a caretaker, I saw him as someone else to take care of. He was horrible to me, but it was better than losing something I had put so much time, effort, heart, and money into.

I didn't have the best relationship with my mom. So when Allan treated me poorly, I thought, *Okay. My mother showed her love this way. Allan acts this way. He must love me!* Well, after two and a half years I finally realize love is not supposed to hurt.

Being a caretaker has made it hard for me to let go. I want to be taken care of! I'm trying to break the pattern of putting others before myself. I did it for so long. Now it's time for me. When I was ready to be taken care of, Allan wasn't ready to care. Losing my mom has made me realize that I need to be my own support, my own guide, my own best friend.

Sherri,

twenty-one, whose mother died after surgery four years ago

I lost my mother, very suddenly, when I was seventeen. She was forty-two when she died of complications from brain surgery that was supposed to remove an aneurysm.

Before my mother died, we were a happy, typical, all-American family living in the Midwest, and I really didn't know how lucky I was. Perhaps I'm being too hard on myself, but when I try to think of memories of me and my mom, I remember that I was a brat much of the time. Everyone assures me that "she knew how much you loved her," but sometimes I wonder. I am stubborn like my father in that I like to handle things myself, without depending on other people. One day I gave in and started to read a book on grief by C. S. Lewis. His theory was that the deceased person for whom we mourn does not look over us for the rest of our lives, as I had been assured. Friends and family repeated, "She'll always be with you," countless times when I was in despair. According to Lewis, this would be too painful for the deceased person, to watch the life that was stolen from them continue without them. This theory troubled me so much that I stopped reading those kinds of do-it-yourself grief books. I knew that I could not survive if I didn't believe that Mom could hear me talk and watch me live.

A favorite comfort of my dad is to tell me that Mom gave me everything I need to live a wonderful life. The way she influenced and loved me in such a short time is more than most people receive in a lifetime. I know this is true, but it never serves as much of a comfort. Why did God take her away when I wasn't done with her yet? I still spend hours trying to find the answer to this question. Maybe some angels needed her warmth and compassion to save thousands of children. No, that's not good enough. I don't care about those children. She's *my* mom. Why couldn't God choose someone else's mother? With all the cruel people in this world who contribute nothing but pain to others, why did God steal a person who embodied the concept of love? I had always lived by the idea that everything happens for a reason. But what could possibly be the reason for this? Was God trying to punish me? There surely were other ways I could learn to do more household chores than to have to do them because Mom is gone. Maybe if Mom had lived, something would have happened to cause her great pain and suffering, so God took her painlessly to prevent that. Today, this is still the explanation that I cling to most often.

Perhaps finding the explanation is less important than learning how to deal with the consequences. I still have faith that Mom is with me everywhere that I go. Sometimes I like to close my eyes and deceive myself into imagining that she is *really* with me. I imagine hugging her again. I picture her visiting me at college with my dad, meeting my roommates and all of the people in my life who will never have the privilege of knowing her. I can't help thinking that if she is watching me from heaven, she is probably very sad to be away. Dad always insists that he never feels sorry for himself, as devastated as he is to have lost his wife. "The person I feel sorry for is your mother," he says, with tears in his eyes. "She doesn't get to be with her children as they grow up."

My constant mourning has lessened over the years, but an incredible fear of death seems to have taken its place. The thought of death horrifies me. My only comfort is the hope that I will be reunited with my mother. This fear of death has begun to play an increasingly important role in how I live my life. It has caused me to think very seriously about what is meaningful. I'll never forget that I was too busy studying to realize that Mom was having surgery the next day. I didn't have the perspective to understand that my schoolwork should have been sacrificed to spend more time with her. Now, the people I love are more important to me than books and papers are. Still, I know a person cannot live entirely by this attitude. I'm constantly debating whether to live for now or to prepare for the future. I suppose every person must find a way to balance the two, but I've never been very good at balancing things.

I'm not sure that I have accepted Mom's death entirely, but I have tried to live as full a life as possible for the past four years, and I'll continue to do so. My father has always encouraged me to look for the positive in every situation. Well, Dad, this is a tough one. Four years later, I still can't come up with even one positive consequence that holds any weight. I have decided, however, that living my life as fully as my mother did, by continuing to use her as my example, is a way to avoid adding to the negativity of her absence.

I continue to be confused, sad, angry, and scared, often all at once. I desperately wish I could speak to her one more time. I can feel her presence beside me now, and I can only have faith that she feels my love.

Not long ago, I wrote her the following letter:

Dear Mom,

How's the weather in heaven? Is it sunny? It's been kind of cloudy lately here. I was just thinking about you and thought I'd write. I really miss you, Mom. My life is going really well and I wish you could be a part of it. The other day I jogged by where you and Dad and I used to live. I was too young to remember that house, but I remember the playground you used to take me to. It seems a lot smaller now. I visited you at the cemetery once around Christmas, and I'm sorry I didn't go again. It's just that I don't picture you there. I picture you alive and with me every day. Please make a special effort to be with me this Monday when I take my exam on the Bible; I could use some inside information. I love you, Mom. Please look over Dad and Paul; I don't think they let you know how they feel as openly as I do. Give my love to Jupiter and Mozart. The house seems empty without Jupiter's barking, and I still miss Mozart's chirping. I feel better knowing they're with you. I envy them for that. Please keep in touch and let me know when you receive this letter—I'm not sure about the postage.

Love always,
Sherri

CHAPTER THREE

Pain Turns to Longing: Five to Ten Years

This is where my personal experience with grieving began. For seven full years after my mother died, I'd managed to neatly bypass sadness, despair, anger, guilt, and remorse. Instead, I'd focused on being the bravest little soldier in my family's army of four. Whenever an intense emotion started to bubble up, I forcefully pushed it back down. The equation was remarkably simple. If I didn't allow myself to think or talk about my mother, I didn't get upset. I learned to react like a mechanical doll that repeated the same sentence every time my string was pulled: "I'm doing fine, thank you."

I've read that losing a loved one is like breaking a bone: without proper treatment the injury will heal on its own, but it won't heal properly. Unless you break and reset the bone, it'll cause you pain for the rest of your life. In much the same way, a daughter who does not or cannot grieve for her mother will be able to function on the surface, but she won't feel emotionally whole again until she revisits the loss and allows herself to feel its accompanying emotional pain.

Gloria Steinem once said that for years she believed she could keep a wall between herself and her childhood, only to discover what a faulty construction that was. Seven years after my mother's death, I found it impossible—and exhausting— to maintain such a division between myself and my grief for any longer. The wall, quite simply, collapsed without warning. Which is how I wound up at the age of twenty-four, doubled over in the middle of a street as cars whizzed by, crying for my mother. On that bright spring afternoon I finally felt what I hadn't been capable of feeling at seventeen.

I've met several motherless women who've also said it took them seven years to start to mourn. Seven-year cycles exist in nature and in social anthropology (such as the "seven-year itch"), but I had to wonder, Why would so many daughters see seven years pass before they begin grieving for a mother? Only when I noticed that all of these women were adolescents at the time of loss did this seven-year lapse seem like more than mere coincidence.

For most teenage daughters who lose their mothers, a five- to ten-year period offers enough time to gain independence from the nuclear family. Many daughters are forced into a state of *emotional* independence after their mothers die but remain financially or socially dependent on their close relatives or caregivers until their early to midtwenties. At that time, they're likely to make the transition to a family or a job of their own and establish a home base that doesn't involve relatives for the first time.

Only when a daughter feels secure within her own life, when she's free from daily ties to her family members and doesn't have to worry about their reactions to her grief (including being cut off from the family for speaking about the unspeakable), will she feel safe enough to mourn. For me, that time arrived during my twenty-fourth year. I'd just experienced another profound loss—the breakup of an engagement—but this time I had a secure job and a close group of friends whom I knew would provide me with a safety net if I stumbled. Mourning the loss of my fiancé and the plans we'd made together sent me right back to mourning for my mother, but this time I was ready to face the pain. Intense emotion felt like much less of a threat to me at twenty-four than it had at seventeen.

The five- to ten-year postloss period carries women who were adolescents and young adults when their mothers died into years that may include marriage, childbirth, and other life transitions that make a motherless woman deeply miss her mother and yearn for her guidance and care. Letters from daughters who lost mothers between five and ten years ago reveal that even adult daughters feel vulnerable and long to be taken care of. They feel the need for mothering now as much as ever, especially when facing the new challenges adulthood brings. Although grief is no longer their daily, constant companion, it now shows up at times of change—happy and sad—and in moments of stress. Thirty-one-year-old Beth Ann, for example, yearned to call her mother four years ago when her first baby died and now longs to call her when she needs advice or reassurance while raising her young daughter.

If a daughter is quite young when her mother died, five or ten years later will find her in the midst of adolescence. An important task of the teen years is to develop an independent identity, and, to achieve this, a girl needs a woman to measure herself against and separate from. When a mother is not present, a daughter may act out against a father or an older sister instead. In addition, the experiences a teen normally would share with her mother—from learning how to manage her first period to shopping for a prom dress—must be shared with another family member or negotiated alone. As thirteen-year-old Gabriella, whose mother died five years ago, explains, "Some people know I don't have a mom and some don't. Her death still bothers me, but usually only when I think about it for a while. I do admit, though, when I see daughters and moms doing things together, I get jealous. I have to do every-thing with my dad. Sometimes that's a bad thing."

Five to ten years after losing their mothers, most daugh-ters have started to identify some positive outcomes that have directly and indirectly resulted from their mother's deaths. Twenty-six-year-old Pamela believes that if her mother hadn't died, she never would have left her hometown, attended grad-uate school, or met the man she is now engaged to marry. Twenty-eight-year-old Cory worked hard to achieve the dream her mother had for her: she earned a college degree.

And yet these achievements are often tinged bittersweet when a mother is not there to witness and share them. For some daughters, the five- to ten-year postloss period marks a shift from focusing on what they themselves have lost to what their mothers have lost by dying. Thirty-two-year-old Mere-dith describes the amazement she feels when she remembers that the mother she nursed through an extended illness will never get to meet her husband or children. Although younger motherless daughters also grieve when they think about future events, the abstract becomes painfully real when these antici-pated moments start to occur.

Five to ten years past a mother's death, daughters often find few resources available to support them with ongoing mourning. Friends and extended family members cannot understand how a death that occurred "so long ago" still causes sadness and emotional pain. True, the acute pain these daughters once felt has diminished. It's been replaced by a dull longing that is more bearable but, in the words of thirty-three-year-old Judy, "never really goes away."

* * *

Pamela,

twenty-six, whose mother died of leukemia five years ago

My mother was my best friend . . . and even more so than the stereotypical mother-daughter best-friend dynamic. I was diagnosed with a hearing loss at three years old and had to wear hearing aids and lip-read to communicate with people. My mother chose to mainstream me in the public school and fought for me every step of the way to ensure I received the education and accommodations necessary. Don't think I was privileged, though. My mom always instilled in me that I wasn't entitled but that I had to work harder than other people.

I am so grateful to her for doing this for me and being a stronger fighter and advocate because it taught me how to fight for myself . . . sooner than I realized I would have to. When I was twenty-one years old and starting my senior year of college, my mom was literally gone in a matter of days. On move-in day, a Friday, my mom was arguing with the residence life staff about accommodations not being in place for my apartment; on Saturday, she was in the hospital; on Monday, she was diagnosed with leukemia; on Tuesday, she started chemotherapy; and on Wednesday, she passed away.

I was completely and utterly devastated. I hadn't even wrapped my mind around the fact that she had cancer before she was gone. My mom, a nurse, must have known she was sicker than we realized because she wrote my brothers and me letters before she died. "Do not let this set you back," she wrote. "I will always be with you in your heart no matter what. Think of me and I will be there!"

I now had to learn how to live without my mother, my best friend, and my biggest advocate. Fortunately, my mother made me strong enough to survive her death, and I feel that her death made me strong enough to survive whatever else that life has to throw at me. That's not to say it wasn't hard. . . . It was incredibly hard and led to the eventual demise of my relationship with my mother's family, much to my regret.

But if I hadn't lost my mother, I probably never would have decided that I needed a career that would get me out of the town I'd lived in my whole life. Although I love my hometown, the memories were too painful, and I wanted to see what else was out there in the world. I ended up getting my master's degree.

Before starting school, I had also made the decision to get a cochlear implant. This was single-handedly the hardest decision that I ever made in my life, and one that was so hard to do without my mother. And now, I am so happy I did it. My hearing increased from 28 percent to 75 percent. My only regret is that my mom, who worked so hard with me on speech therapy and fought so hard for me, wasn't there to see me hear with the implant for the first time and hasn't been here to see the progress I've made since. But I also know that I never would have had the courage to do it and to put in the rehabilitative work it has required without the strength she gave me.

While I was in graduate school, I reconnected with a man I'd graduated from high school with and made the snap decision to move in with him after only a couple of months. "Hey, I could die tomorrow," was my philosophy. We got engaged after six months. My mother would have been so worried as a bystander here on earth, but I know that, looking down from heaven, she was so happy for me.

I got my master's degree, and within months my fiancé and I moved out west. I am now a cowgirl! This is something that never would have happened had my mother lived. I don't know that I would have considered graduate school or moving or even dating a divorced man with children, and we are still together three amazing years later.

I am beyond happy and so grateful for the things that have led me to where I am now: living with my fiancé, being involved in his children's lives, and working in a job that allows me to help others suffering from setbacks and losses in their lives. I take chances and love fully and live hungrily. I can stand on my own two feet without my fiancé or anyone else, all because my mother taught me that I needed to be able to provide for myself. She may not have told me what I needed to do for a career, but indirectly her death showed me the path that I needed to follow.

Not a day goes by when I don't miss her, but I have learned I need to live my life without her in it and not hold myself back from amazing experiences just because my mom isn't here to live her life as well. That is the last thing she would have wanted for me. Today, one of the best compliments I can receive is that I'm just like my mother: "You really are Linda's daughter!" is one of my favorite sentences.

Beth Ann,

thirty-one, whose mother died of colon cancer seven years ago

To me, the hardest time to be a motherless daughter was when I lost my first child four years ago. It was the worst possible situation—I was twenty-six weeks along and was on an overnight business trip three hours from home. I had been feeling fine but started feeling "sick" in the evening. By the time I decided it was premature labor and my doctor had told me to get to the nearest hospital as soon as possible, I was near panic. Three hours from home, from my doctors, and especially from my husband and father, I *really* needed my mother to talk to. I spent three days in a strange hospital (my husband and father had rushed down that night) while strange doctors worked to stop my premature labor. I kept thinking over and over, "If I could just talk to my mom, maybe I wouldn't be so afraid." After I lost the baby, my dad tried to comfort me, but I really needed my mom there, to have someone who had gone through the same thing tell me why I should want to keep living.

I got pregnant with my daughter just three months later, but I spent my entire pregnancy afraid of every twinge of discomfort. Until my daughter was at least eighteen months old, I checked her several times a night to make sure she was still breathing. I've lost count of the many nights I fell asleep crying, saying to my husband, "If only I could talk to my mom, ask her opinions, find out just how she felt in these situations."

I had a lot of trouble really bonding with my daughter. I was overwhelmed with the responsibility after I had her, and

I didn't have my mother around to compare notes with. I've tried talking to my mother-in-law, but it's just not the same. I want to be able to just call up my mother and say, "So, how did *you* handle tantrums?"

I've tried talking to others, especially my dad, when I have a question or need advice, but I think I haven't really coped all that well. Since my mother's death I've turned to compulsive overeating whenever my emotions overwhelm me. Lately I've begun exercising regularly to reduce some of the stress, but I've still got a long way to go. I'm seeing a therapist for this and related problems.

I don't cry as much anymore, but still hardly a day goes by that I don't wish I could just talk to her, even one more time.

Judy,

thirty-three, whose mother died of pancreatic cancer eight years ago

We buried my mother, who was forty-six, the day before my twenty-fifth birthday. My youngest sister was fourteen years old, and my parents were newly divorced at the time of my mother's death. I became the guardian of my younger sister and raised her until she went away to college. The first words she said to me after we returned home from the hospital after our mom died were "don't make me go with him," meaning my father. I became a pseudomom to my sister, and although it was the most challenging and difficult thing I have done in my life so far, I would do it again.

I still do not have a healthy relationship with my father, who is remarried. I believe my sisters and I get along better with our stepmother than we do with him. The interesting thing about my father is that he carries so much guilt about my mother that I doubt he will ever get past that so he can finally grieve for her. We are constant reminders of her to him, which poses one of the problems between my father and his daughters.

Today I am a mom and have a wonderful son who will be two years old in September. Yes, I expected to have a daughter but am elated to have a boy. The bond I have with him is strong, and he does fill the void somewhat, as does marriage. But the hole in my heart never really goes away. It amazes me that it has been eight years since my mom left us and I still get the same feeling you did when you cried, "I want my mother."

It overcomes me without warning. My wedding day and the day I gave birth were probably two of the most emotionally mixed days I have ever experienced. I found that the joy and the sadness have a weird way of mixing together, and what a struggle that is.

One of the only things that hasn't made me insane is that I know my mother is no longer in pain or suffering and is in a much better place. She is always with me, and her voice rings in the back of my head. But oh, what I wouldn't do to have *one second* just to touch her and have her with me for a moment.

Sandy,

thirty-eight, whose mother died of brain cancer eight and a half years ago

I lost my mother eight and a half years ago, and sometimes it feels as if it happened only yesterday. My mother was and still is the best friend I ever had. When she was diagnosed with incurable brain cancer, I was thirty years old and the mother of three daughters, ages three, two, and one. I fortunately lived only a couple of miles away and was able to be with my mother constantly. Every morning I took my three girls and went over to spend the day with her. I cleaned, cooked, shopped, helped her shower and go to the bathroom, and read to her. My children made her laugh. I am lucky to have a wonderful husband who did whatever he could to make things better for us all. My two brothers and my sister came by daily to break the monotony. I had the days, and my dad had the nights. He was completely devoted to her. For a year, this was our life. People would ask, "How can you do this to your children?" My answer was, I was doing it *for* my children. They truly learned about love, compassion, and hope.

When my mother died two weeks after her fifty-second birthday, she was in her own home. All her children and my father were around her bed as she quietly slipped away. My daughters had all napped in the same bed with her earlier that day. It was close to midnight, and my father and I wouldn't let them take her to the funeral home until the next morning. We sat by her bed all night, although one of my siblings couldn't bear it and stayed in another room. Daddy and I had been with her every moment of the way, and we weren't willing to let her go yet.

As my father and I sat there talking, I realized that I was still alive. I had truly thought that when my mother died, I would too. It was during that long night that I knew the best thing I could do for my mother was to go on and be the kind of person she always wanted me to be. I have grieved for almost nine years and always will. There is not a single day that goes by when my mother is not on my mind. My youngest daughter is named after her; my house holds her things; she is in my soul; my mother is me.

Last year I lost a very good friend at the age of thirty-eight to breast cancer. She had struggled for five years. Adele left behind two daughters, seven and four years old. The cancer had been discovered when she was pregnant with her second. We became close only after she got sick. Adele was able to confide her true feelings to me because she knew if I could handle my mother's death, I could handle anything.

Today, I have a wonderful life. My husband is the best, and my girls are healthy, happy, and beautiful. I live in a very strong, supportive community. I have friends that have been there for me for years and a full life. I help my husband run our business and am active in many organizations. Because of my mother, I do the very best I can for those around me.

Our lives have all been touched, for good and bad. The pain will never go away, but we do go on.

Cory,

twenty-eight, whose mother died of cervical cancer nine years ago

My mother died when she was forty-three and I was nineteen. To this day, I continue to miss her. My mother was a poor, uneducated single parent living in a low-income housing project. We survived on state assistance and received medical care at rural clinics.

I am the youngest of her five children. As my mother was dying, I was struggling to care for her full time and attend the local city college on limited funds. She chose to die at home, in the projects, with the care of her children. I went from seeing an active, proud mother to seeing a helpless, weak young woman who had had a hard life but who continued to be extremely proud of her children's accomplishments.

Today, I'm married with no children. I was educated at a state university, and received a bachelor's degree in social work. I work in the child protection field. The loss of my mother and the loss of my father just two months ago have left me feeling empty and yet proud of what I come from. I think the drive to get an education and be successful that my mother instilled in her children is what keeps me strong and invested in women's issues.

Lynn,

twenty-six, whose mother died of breast cancer nine years ago

My mother died when I was seventeen. She was a single parent, and I was an only child. We lived alone.

My mother was the driving force behind my success as a child. I excelled in academics, and from the sixth grade to the twelfth grade I had full scholarships at the most prestigious private schools in the state. I was a very good dancer and actress—at age fourteen, I was an apprentice with the state ballet. I was pretty, smart, and talented, and my mother and grandmother were very proud of me.

I have never felt as pretty or smart or talented as I was as a child. It took me five and a half years to complete college with a barely average grade point average. Instead of being a theater major and dealing with the heavy competition, I took an easier way out. I did a lot of drugs and was promiscuous. In other words, without my mother pushing me along, I really had no idea how to push myself, how to praise myself, how to be myself.

I guess I've spent a lot of time feeling like my mother was the foundation to my success, and when she died my foundation was pulled out from beneath me. I've been living on some very shaky ground. I've only very recently been learning how to build my own solid foundation. It's very difficult because not only am I a motherless daughter, but I'm also fatherless, grandmotherless, and sister- and brotherless.

In the past, people have described me as very defensive. But now I think my emotions have leveled out, and I'm no longer in so much denial about everything. So I'm coping much better—most of the time.

Sarah,

thirty-nine, whose mother died of cancer nine years ago

My mother was a young and vibrant fifty-seven-year-old when she died, even after having fought cancer for six years with monthly treatments, daily medications, and worsening CT scans. She never gave up. She never lost her bright toothy smile or the twinkle in her light blue eyes.

I tried to hold on to her upbeat attitude in the days, weeks, and months immediately following her death. When she was sick, she told me to never use her illness as a crutch. I was to go on with my life, do my job, and be a contributing member of society. It wasn't easy and sometimes nearly impossible. I had a nine-month-old son to care for, a husband who tried to help me but couldn't, a newly widowed father who I felt very responsible for, and a brother who needed me more than I needed him.

Remarkably, life did go on. I dreaded the big firsts—first holidays, anniversaries, everything that marked the passing of time without my mother. But I discovered that those calendar dates seemed no different from any other days. Many friends and family members called me on what would have been her fifty-eighth, fifty-ninth, and even sixty-fifth birthdays, but to me they were just days. I miss her *every* day.

What I wasn't prepared for were the little moments of missing her, like the day I took my six-year-old daughter shopping for a dress for the father-daughter dance at school. I wept out loud in the dressing room watching her try on the items.

My smiley, light-blue-eyed daughter is named for my dead mother whom she never knew. I felt the loss of my mother for me, for my daughter, and most especially I felt what my mother was missing out on. Shopping was a tradition in our family—a ritual that bonded my mother and me perhaps more than anything else we did together. I can't even imagine how much my mother would have loved to shop for this little girl of mine.

I found myself drawn to a nursing home where my mother had volunteered for many years. At first, I wanted to be there just because she had been, but then I began to see why she wanted to be there. I began fundraising for the home and now run an event every year named in my mother's memory.

I started to practice yoga and meditation. I listened more to others and to myself. I learned to enjoy the time that I have with my father, my brother, and of course my husband, children, other family members and friends. I know all of those clichés too well. Life is not a dress rehearsal; it goes fast, and you never know what's going to happen—good or bad. I have my moments. I yell at my kids, and, when I do, I hear my mother's yelling voice, then can't help but smile. I sometimes feel sorry for myself and for my kids, wondering what our world will be like without a mother and a grandmother. But I try not to go there. It really doesn't do any good.

As I look back, I see a very different and unexpected twist in my life that all started with the loss of my mother. I am much more independent than many of my other young mom friends who rely on their mothers for childcare and advice. I laugh sometimes to make myself feel better, realizing that I don't have to take that unwanted advice.

The truth is that I wish my mother was here for all of it. To give me the unwanted advice, experience the joy of grandparenthood, and allow me to still be her daughter. I know that, had my mother lived, I never would have known many of the wonderful people that have crossed my path since her death. I would not be as self-motivated or grown up. I wish I was a much less self-actualized person with a living mother, but I know I don't have a choice. I go on every day, remembering her, missing her, loving her, and never, never using her as a crutch.

Jacqueline,

thirty-two, whose mother died of a self-inflicted gunshot wound after a long battle with cancer nine years ago

I've had your book for eight years and haven't managed to get all the way through it yet. Within the first paragraph I start crying so hard that I can't see.

My mother had breast cancer and chose not to take medication. I watched the cancer eat away at her until she realized she was losing her mind. She would morph back into a situation from twenty years ago and then within minutes come right back to the present. She finally took her own life three weeks before my twenty-third birthday. She weighed seventy-seven pounds the day she died and didn't want to die in a hospital on machines. I closed her eyes at the morgue that day and still remember the smile she had on her face. I believe she went peacefully, and, having watched so many others die of cancer in hospitals, I know why she took her own life. It was to save me, her only child, from watching her suffer. After all, she too had watched her father die of cancer when she was twenty-three.

I now have a daughter of my own yet find myself in so many situations where I want my own mother. As childish and silly as it sounds, I have a breakdown about every six months. This last one was really hard. I found myself sobbing uncontrollably last week at work, forcing me to leave and go home. I had no real explanation for why my heart had suddenly filled with pain. I found myself, at age thirty-one, curled into a ball in my bedroom screaming into a pillow, "I want my mommy." I don't feel so silly after reading other people's stories.

I don't suppose the pain will ever totally subside. My daughter will be eight in May and still I have a hard time being happy on Mother's Day. I wish it would come and go with no mention. Even though I haven't made it through the book in its entirety yet, the first part has helped me understand more about what these waves of emotion are.

Meredith,

thirty-two, whose mother died of cancer ten years ago

One week ago was the ten-year anniversary of my mother's death. She died two days after my twenty-second birthday. (To this day, I believe she held out for those two days so she wouldn't die on or so close to my birthday.) I am thirty-two now and finally realize I have a loss and a pain that will never leave me. (So it only took me ten years to realize this; okay, I'm a bit slow.) I cared for my mother for nineteen months with very little support from the rest of my family. To tell you that it was a very difficult time doesn't really come close to what it was like.

The memories that I have not let myself remember for a long time came flooding back to me as I read your book. The day my mother went to take a shower after being in the hospital for more than a week, it was all she talked about. What we didn't realize was that she was too weak to have one alone until she stood there naked and shivering in the bathroom. Her eyes filled with tears. She looked like a child would look to an adult, silently pleading for me to help her. Without thinking, I jumped into the shower, fully clothed, and held her arms for support. She started to wash, and then, realizing what I had done, she began to laugh. We were laughing so hard that my father knocked on the door asking if we were all right, which only made us laugh harder.

There was the day I went into her hospital room and she handed me her hairbrush and asked me to help her. She couldn't stand the fact that, every time she moved her head, clumps of hair would fall out. I brushed and brushed, hiding my horror as her beautiful, dark hair fell into my hands. She didn't cry, not one tear. When I finished, a bald woman thanked me and said, "There, that's done."

I held my mother's hand when she died. My sister and both of our best friends were also in the room. I watched her last breath, still unsure as I asked my sister, "Is she? . . ." "Yes," my sister whispered. I immediately looked up to the ceiling, expecting to see her soul. Later as I sat alone with her body, I studied her fingers and hands. She had the most beautiful hands.

A few months after my mother died, I had been out one night with a boy I dated before my mother got sick. We went to the beach to see the sunrise. I came home to find my father sitting at our dining room table with his head in his hands, crying. This was the first time I had ever seen my father cry. Panic seized me: I thought someone else had died. I was shocked when he told me he was worried because he didn't know where I was. When I was growing up, my father had been very much the absent father. As he was organizing the first peace movement march in our town during the Vietnam War, my mother was teaching me to swim, driving me to tennis lessons, and listening to the problems a ten-year-old has. My mother set curfews, as well as the other rules in our house. After my mother died, it never, not once, occurred to me to let my dad know where I was when I went out. So here sat my father, basically a stranger to me, crying and telling me,

"Meredith, I just don't know how it works." I explained that before Mom had gotten sick, she and I had a very trusting relationship, and I would call her if I was going to be out past midnight. I would tell her where I was and who I was with. She'd let me know if she was comfortable with that. She knew my friends, and it was almost never a problem. Even then, my dad could not set rules on his own. He asked me in disbelief, "You call at midnight? You don't come home then?" (This man was my father for twenty-two years; how could he not have known this?)

My father was devastated when a few months later I told him I would be moving to the Midwest. He never understood that I moved across the United States to leave the role of caretaker that my family immediately gave me, the youngest child. I have two older brothers and one sister, who were all grown and out of the house when I was growing up. Each one has his or her own demons and was unable to cope with my mother's illness. Out of the three, only my sister and I have any contact. There was a lot of damage done during those years my mother was ill. My sister resented the fact that I was able to cope, and I still cannot forgive her that she couldn't. When I was little, I idolized my sister. So the devastation I felt when she abandoned my mother and me was immense. When she finally had the courage to come around, the damage had been done. My mother had grown unbelievably dependent on me. I remember when my sister went to help my mother one day and my mother said, "No, we must ask Meredith. . . . She knows how to." I will never forget the hatred in my sister's eyes. To this day, it is there between us.

In the nineteen months my mother lived with cancer, I had five days off. I flew to Chicago to see a good friend. We went to a club, and I danced with a college student I met. I told him everything he wanted to know about me except for one small detail: that I took care of my mother, who was dying from cancer. I let him believe I was nothing other than a twenty-two-year-old visiting her friend. The depression was so severe when I had to leave, I didn't think I would be physically able to get on the plane. (Maybe it was the look my mother acquired in her eyes that I could no longer bear. She had been cheated out of her life, and she knew it. As each month passed, a bit of my mother slipped away till I hardly recognized the woman I was caring for.) When I got home, my mother had left little notes on my bed welcoming me back and telling me funny little details that went on while I was gone. She came to the door of my room, wanting to hear all about my trip. I didn't even hug her. I rushed past her and was sick in our bathroom. I was so upset and angry at the fact that I wasn't that girl I pretended to be on my trip. I was a young girl who had come home to watch her mother deteriorate in front of her eyes. All of my friends had gone off to universities and had their whole lives to look forward to. I had nothing to look forward to but watching my mother die. But worse was the cold treatment I had toward her that day. She was hurt by it, and I couldn't stop. I was as bad as my sister, who had deserted her in the beginning; it just took me a little longer. This memory still haunts me. If I was granted any day in my entire life to relive, it would be that day.

After quite a few painful relationships, I met the man I knew I would marry five years ago. We were married last summer. It still seems unreal to me that my mother never got to meet him. I have no doubt in my mind they would have quickly become friends. It amazes me that this is the man I plan to spend the rest of my life with and he has never heard my mother's laughter or seen the sparkle in her eyes when her sense of humor was at its best. I alternate between disbelief that she is not here to see my life as an adult and anger that I have been cheated out of hearing her say to me, *What a great guy he is. You sure had me worried, kiddo, with all those years of surfers coming through the door. And you marry a European— who would have thought!*

A wonderful woman I met years ago while caring for my grandmother told me that no one would ever love me like my mother did. It still brings tears to my eyes when I remember her telling me this. This quest I have been on to fill the void has brought up three older women in my life who are my surrogate mothers. Each one reminds me of my own mother in one way or another. The woman I have known the longest and am closest to was my "mother for the day" on my wedding day. Just before I was to walk into the church, she hugged me and whispered, "Your mother is right here beside you, you sweet child. Don't think she isn't." I firmly believe this—that my mother is beside me and inside me and always will be. I refuse to forget her. Maybe the sound of her voice has faded from my memory, but the love she gave me, the sense of humor she passed on to me, and the sense of integrity that she possessed are here waiting for me to pass on to my child, when I find the courage to have one.

When I was eighteen, I moved away from home. My mom gave me a travel alarm clock with a card that is now framed and in my bathroom. I read it each morning. "To Meredith, to wish you the best of time in the future, to keep you on time for all of your appointments, and to remind you that I love you all of the time. Mother." I know my mother and I would have been friends if she had lived. I know that she would be proud of me at times and disappointed in me as well. (With all my travels and adventures, going to a university was not one of them. To this day, wherever she is, I'll bet that bothers her.) But I also know she would love me unconditionally, like only a mother can, like only my mother did.

CHAPTER FOUR

Experience Turns to Insight: Ten to Twenty Years

By the ten-year point, most daughters have shifted their focus toward the lasting effects of mother loss. They mourn the absence of support and advice they believe their mothers would have provided, especially at times of change such as marriage, childbirth, and divorce. The daughter who has been without a mother for this long tends to romanticize and idealize the potential of their lost relationship, often imagining her mother's presence as a cure-all for her current woes.

One of the motherless woman's most challenging long-term tasks of mourning is to develop a realistic picture of her mother, to adopt the qualities she admires, and to reject the rest. All daughters must do this to some degree, but the daughter with a living mother has accessible images—both Good Mother and Bad Mother—she can accept and reject. The daughter who's lost her mother has to piece together her image through memory and investigative research. When the mother has been idealized or sanctified, which frequently happens after a loved one dies, the daughter has no Bad Mother to resist. When she focuses only on her mother's good traits, she creates an unrealistic and impossible standard for herself to achieve.

In this chapter, we see daughters who lost their mothers between ten and twenty years ago searching for ways to keep the memory of the Good Mother, as well as their connections to her, alive. Twenty-nine-year-old Maggie, whose mother died eleven years ago, writes about the "ongoing conversations" they continue to have. Thirty-four-year-old Phoebe has done genealogical research on her mother's family, trying to develop and maintain a connection to all her maternal relatives.

In this chapter we also read women's accounts of what psychologists call "arrested development." This occurs when parts of a child's emotional development freeze at the time of a childhood trauma such as mother loss. Some daughters describe feeling as if their personalities have split. They go through the motions of their peer group yet still feel like children inside. As twenty-three-year-old Robbie, who was five when her mother died of cancer, explains:

> On the one hand, I'm a very responsible and mature person for my age. I've been working and studying full time for four years. A lot of people I know tell me that I'm the oldest young person they know, which I find funny but ironic. The irony is in the fact that so often I feel as though I'm still a little girl, still five years old, very scared and shy and without a mother, always a little lost and feeling as though I'm on the outside looking in.

At the same time that women like Robbie draw connections between long-term difficulties and their early mother loss, they also write of their resilience and self-pride. These daughters have experienced the most traumatic loss a young child can imagine and have survived. Armed with this knowledge, many motherless women believe they can face virtually any adverse event in the future and persevere. As forty-one-year-old Natalie, who was seventeen when her mother died, so succinctly says, "I fear nothing because I've already lost everything."

Also notable in this chapter are the number of daughters who made sure to include their mothers' exact ages at time of death. It may be that the ten- to twenty-year period starts bringing daughters closer to the mother's age when she died, making them more acutely aware of just how young their mothers were. As daughters themselves move further into adulthood and its related roles, they begin to identify more strongly with their mothers as professional women, wives, and mothers. By doing so, they gain a broader perspective of who their mothers were as individuals and also how much of life they missed out on because they died so young. This new awareness is sometimes accompanied by a new mourning cycle—another reminder that even ten or fifteen or twenty years after a mother's death, the processes of re-evaluation and adaptation continue on.

• • •

Maggie,

twenty-nine, whose mother died of cancer eleven years ago

My mother died when I was eighteen, and I had not really begun to give deep thought to her death's effect on me until I read about the continuing conversations that motherless daughters have with their mothers long after their death. This does not necessarily mean talking to an image but is usually a search for an answer to "What would she have liked me to do?" There are two "conversations" I've had with my mother that I'd like to share.

The first came right after my mother passed away, and I was given the task of deciding what clothes to dress her in for burial. The responsibility fell on my shoulders, as I was the younger sister of two older brothers and thus the only female left in the immediate family. I had, of course, no experience in picking out clothes for interment. What does one choose? The most comfortable and attractive clothing for the hereafter? Would my mother's ghost be forever regretting the outfit I chose for her?

I decided that she would've killed me if I buried anything good. I could hear her saying, *Of all things, why would you put a Perry Ellis blazer in a coffin for eternity? You could still get good use from it.* I then thought I'd pick a dress that she'd worn at one of the happier times in her life. She had lived with cancer for six years prior to her death, so it would have to have been before the time she became sick.

I chose the dress she wore on the day of my brother's graduation. It was a typical midseventies dress, so it wasn't "too good" for burial, but she'd worn it at a happy occasion—the accomplishment of one of her children. No one questioned my choice. I still don't know why. When I look back at this now, I can't believe the thought that went into this decision, particularly for an eighteen-year-old. But, then again, she helped me make the decision.

A second ongoing conversation I still have is whether or not to visit her grave. The only time after the funeral that I have been there was a year after her death. One of the positive results of my mother's death is a profound appreciation for those people who are still here. As a result, my focus that day at her grave was on how nice it was to be holding my father's arm and looking at the blank space next to my mother's name on the headstone.

I have not been back to her grave since. I feel that it wouldn't do much good to remember my mother by staring at her grave. If I want to visit her spirit, I am much better off going clothes shopping at Loehmann's. We shared many wonderful times there that could only be shared with a daughter. Loehmann's was also the place where she went for "therapy." For now, I've decided that visiting my mother's grave is not something she would have wanted me to do. She would have preferred that I carry on her spirit by living an independent, happy life, as she taught me to do by words and example. I can remember her or speak to her anywhere and often do.

Some women who've lost their mothers say they needed to see their mothers' bodies after death, to say a proper good-bye.

I never wanted to see my mother without life. As I mentioned, I'd lived with my mother and her cancer for six years before she died. I'd learned to express my love for her whenever I felt it. I didn't need to see my mother's body for closure. I didn't want to have a memory of what she looked like after death. She hadn't, in fact, looked like herself for some time. The disease and her medication had altered her appearance. In the last month of her life, the surgery on her brain, where the cancer had finally spread after beginning in her breast, had almost completely taken away her ability to communicate. So, just as I'd chosen not to helplessly ride behind the ambulance taking her to the hospital or enter her hospital room after she died or see her in her coffin, I chose instead to live with the memories of my mother full of life, and not without it.

Deena,

twenty-six, whose mother committed suicide twelve years ago

My mother committed suicide when I turned fourteen. She was forty-three. She might have benefited from your book, because she had lost her mother to suicide at a young age. My grandmother also was forty-three when she died. Mommy was fourteen at the time. I guess she never really got over it, worked through it, or accepted it. Those twenty-nine years in between were somewhat of a living hell for her. Or so I imagine.

I've been writing in a journal for years, and it isn't always easy. But it's the best gift I could have given myself—the gift of sanity. No, I'm not depressed or suicidal or unhappy, but you just reaffirmed for me that all of us "mother-challenged" (if you're into political correctness, which I am *not*) girls go through this. Or parts of it. And we make it just fine. Some of us actually lead normal lives . . . but we do feel that, to a certain degree, we *are* different.

My friend Elaine and I got to know each other shortly after I moved to the Midwest for my job. She showed up at my firm. Slim and beautiful, she walked past our receptionist, who commented on how thin she was getting. I asked Nina if she could tell me the secret to Elaine's slimness, and Nina said that her mother had been diagnosed with cancer, and that's why Elaine moved back to town, to spend whatever time her mother had left with her.

I had never met Elaine, but I sent her a note letting her know that I had lost my mother and that I could probably relate—and that I could certainly provide two ears and two shoulders. A few days later, Elaine and I went to lunch, cried over a Caesar salad, and became friends. That was two years ago, and I don't think we'll ever lose touch, even though I now live more than five hundred miles away.

Because I'm only twenty-six, I still have seventeen years to get to that "fated" forty-three. It's a year, I'm sure, which will be pretty uneventful for me, because the biggest lesson I learned from a grandmother I never met and a mother I forgave is that life, this life, *my life*, is tremendously fun and worth living.

Hannah,

nineteen, whose mother died of breast cancer twelve years ago

My mother died when I was seven years old. I came across your book online having been searching for something like it for a while now. To understand that I am not alone or stupid for feeling the way I do was a relief to me. I now see that, like the other women, I never grieved the death and have never gotten over it. I just shut off and don't think about it. However, I now don't know what to do. I feel lost. I feel like I have no one to talk to, not because I don't want to but because I can't.

After reading the book, which I did in about two days, I shut down, turned my phone off and stayed in bed for three days. My boyfriend fell out with me for a few days, and even then I could not bring myself to tell him the real reason for my distance. I don't know how to talk about it and never have, mainly because it is just never spoken about in the family. My dad recently got engaged to his long-term partner, and it seems that everyone has managed to move on apart from me being left behind all alone.

Your book shows me that perhaps there is light at the end of the tunnel. I just need to take the first steps. My friend went through the same thing when her mother died, but I don't feel like I can even speak to her. I wish I could tell my boyfriend and my friends why I am so distant but I just can't seem to say the words. Saying them out loud makes them real, and I don't want them to be real. It seems strange to grieve a death now that happened twelve years ago. How can I explain that to people?

Even if I cannot face my own family and friends with this, I have found all these other women [in the book] who understand the feeling and that is the support system I have always needed. I have next to no childhood memories of my mother; I seem to have blocked them out, which is greatly upsetting to me. One of the more horrible things I remember following the death was when another girl in my class's father died, and one of the other children said to me, "She has it worse because your dad is the fun one." It completely disregarded the death of a mother as devastating.

Losing my mother has meant I have also lost myself. I have found so much comfort in the fact that I am not stupid for my feelings because all motherless daughters have similar thoughts. All my friends say I am the strongest person they know, but behind the scenes, where no one can see me, I am falling apart. Thank you for helping me see I am not alone.

Melanie,

thirty-two, whose mother died of ovarian cancer twelve years ago

My parents waited to tell us about my mother's cancer. For whatever reason, they felt the need to shelter my high-school-aged brother and me from the harsh reality that lay before her. I remember the sit-down family meeting when they told us. I don't think I was too worried at the time. My mom was invincible, and she would continue to show us over the next few years just how resilient she was.

She had a complete hysterectomy to remove the grapefruit-sized tumor she'd discovered in her uterus one day when she pressed on her lower abdomen and realized it didn't budge the way it should. They did what they could to remove the cancer that had found its way into her lymph nodes. She underwent chemotherapy, but ultimately it didn't define her life—just another appointment to add in her already jam-packed datebook. She was still the loud, straightforward teacher that I'd always known her to be, who cherished my brother and me. I had the privilege of cutting her hair into a Mohawk right before we buzzed it all off. We went wig shopping together. She made lifestyle changes to help improve her potential outcome, eating cleaner foods and reading books on how to discourage cancer cells from taking a hold of her body. We learned that her cancer was gone, hurray!

Unfortunately, in the time that we spent celebrating a clean bill of health, her cancer traveled up her spinal cord and into her brain, where it took root and continued to grow.

We had to hold her down that night that we took her to the hospital, disoriented and unaware of the breakdown occurring in her body. This turn of fate led her to radiation therapy and then to direct injections into a port in her skull, with the hope that she might respond positively. I cried that night at the computer when I realized that I wanted my mother to die because I knew that she would never be the same. She would never again do any of those things she enjoyed—sewing, shopping, teaching. She would tell visitors that she was coming back to the classroom soon, but we knew she would never walk out our front door again.

My brother and I were never told that my mom had less than a 20 percent chance of living past five years. She battled for three and a half before she couldn't fight anymore. I was twenty.

It was the single most defining moment of my young life, and I still considered myself lucky. I was lucky to have always been close with my mother, to keep her close during my teenage years, to have the beginnings of an adult relationship with her, even though it was cut short. So many other motherless daughters were never as blessed as I was, to have spent twenty good years with their mother. Still, it pained me to watch those around me take their mother for granted—to bicker and fight about the most inconsequential of topics. I would give anything to have my mom still here, even if it was for a spat. The most important person in my life was gone.

With my world rocked I was desensitized. Later that year I watched as the news aired the planes crashing into the World

Trade Center. What shook so many people in this country barely registered with me. They lost loved ones? Welcome to the tragic reality I'd lived with for the past seven months.

The grieving process has been ongoing for me, as it has been for any motherless daughter. It doesn't get easier, but it does get better. I've learned to be thankful for mother figures in my life and to help put things in perspective for my friends. Appreciation takes on a new level of understanding and depth when you have loss as a frame of reference. With loss came life in the form of a closer bond to my father, who stepped into the role of confidante, the one who truly knows how to read every nuance in the tone of my voice.

I still feel the loss of my mother every day. That grief doesn't go away but takes new shape, transforming with the changes in my life. I wonder what she would've done, what she would've said, and if she would've approved. I have no way of knowing, and I try to hold onto the faith that she would've supported my decisions.

I became a mother to a daughter when I reached thirty-two, a year older than my mom was when she had me. Post-partum hormones brought with them a rush of grief, as I braced myself against the washing machine that first night home, heaving sobs as I finally comprehended the nature of unconditional love for my daughter, knowing that I had been loved with the same passion. A woman who would never meet my daughter, who would never be there to be a grandma to my daughter, loved me.

My mother has been gone for more than a third of my life by now. She never saw me graduate from college, let alone graduate school. I was never able to call on her for advice during those first few years when I struggled in the workplace. I couldn't seek her input when I made the choice to leave my first husband or the hurried decision to marry my second. She never cheered for me when I made my commitment to our country and enlisted in the military. She was never at the other end of the phone during my pregnancy when I needed her, nor could she provide the wisdom and advice that comes from experience. I brought my daughter into this world without her by my side, barely surviving those first few weeks as an exhausted, fumbling new mom.

That little girl that sleeps in my bed, waiting for me to join her, to nourish her, and to hold her tight—I pray that she never knows this loss, that she never has to seek out this community, and that she never has to learn to function without me as her greatest supporter. She deserves better. I deserved better.

Natalie,

thirty-one, whose mother died of anorexia and alcoholism fourteen years ago

My journey on this road began fourteen years ago, just after Thanksgiving, when my Mother slipped into a coma. At seventeen, I found the very thing I feared most coming true.

That evening, my mother, who had been suffering from anorexia and alcoholism, collapsed on her living room floor. My two younger sisters were getting ready for bed upstairs. My eleven-year-old sister went downstairs to ask our mother a question and discovered her lifeless body. Panicking, she called the paramedics. Arriving thirty minutes later, they were able to resuscitate. My mother had gone into cardiac arrest, and, because her heart had been down for so long, the doctors said she suffered severe brain damage. The only functionality she had left was the ability to breathe on her own every thirty seconds or so. If the choice was made to keep her alive, she would have been on life support with little brain function and no quality of life.

The most difficult part was the not knowing whether she was "still in there." When I visited her in the hospital, I would kiss her on the cheek and tell her I loved her. Tears streamed down her face. Fourteen years later, this thought haunts me still. What if? What if she was screaming in there, unable to let us know she was awake? The what ifs could cripple me. I learned a valuable lesson there. I must learn to keep going straight forward and not dwell on what I cannot control or change.

My mother remained in a coma for two weeks before the family decided to let her go. She was strong. She fought hard. When they predicted she would live a few hours more, she lived for a whole day. But she lost her battle.

She was forty-one.

The aftermath was a blur. Two things consumed me. The first was denial. I would see a woman in the grocery store from behind who had the same hairstyle and would follow her around until I could catch a good glimpse of her face. Even then I'd try to study it. Maybe she'd faked her own death, maybe my family had lied to me. I played these stories out in my head for a few years, even though I fully knew she was gone.

The second and more painful part was dealing with the strained relationship my mother and I had toward the end. I had left home at sixteen to live with my boyfriend. I thought he was trying to save me from the discord at home, but he wanted me away from my family and all to himself. I was too angry with the dysfunction at home to see this. Both of my parents were alcoholics, and I never really had much of a relationship with my father. He was a provider and present in our lives but never wanted the role of fatherhood. He abused my mother both physically and verbally, and verbally abused me.

Alcohol turned my mother into someone else. She wasn't the same fun-loving woman any more. She grew mean. A few stressful events at home, and I was out.

I would later regret this decision, as I felt I failed my mother and my sisters. After my parents divorced my mother moved out and was scraping by to provide for her little ones.

Just a few months prior to my mother's coma, her mother passed away. This was very difficult for my family and would prove to be the end for my mother. At the rate she was spiraling downhill, we knew she might not survive this.

I felt surrounded by death. It was all I thought about. I became a hypochondriac and suffered massive anxiety attacks that left me in a haze for a good six months. I thought I was dying. To this very day, I wonder if I'll make it ten more years to forty-one. What if I outlive my mother?

I've come a long way from those days, but I still find myself comparing my life to my mother's at every age. For example: At thirty-one, my mother had a seven-year-old and a two-year-old, and she and my father had purchased their first home.

At thirty-one, I have no children, nor do I own my own home. I married that abusive boyfriend at twenty-one, and divorced five years later. That's when my "true" self-discovery began. I say this because, while I was with my first husband, I felt imprisoned. I wasn't allowed to breathe. I wasn't allowed to have friendships. I was trapped and severely depressed for ten years. Then, one day . . . I left.

My life began again. I was making it on my own, had a great job, and was free. I had more self-confidence and strength than I'd ever known. I knew I'd made my mother proud. I'm now engaged to a wonderful man who treats me like a goddess and who loves me unconditionally. This is a first for me in a romantic relationship. And yet I still struggle with trusting that I won't lose this one, too.

The things I've endured and learned have left me with an amazing will to live. I fear nothing because I have already lost everything. And that's okay, because I've realized that I've actually gained a lot more than I've lost. I say "lost" lightly, because I do not see my mother's passing as a loss. It was her time. I believe everything that happens, happens for a reason, whether or not we understand. Some things are on too grand a scale for us to understand. That is why there is no end to our learning here on earth.

Who am I today? I now find myself to be a strong woman who is still coming to terms with the fact that you can lose the good things, the most important things, and still stand. I still wake up every morning and am grateful to be able to hear the birds chirp. Everything in my life has meaning, and I'm not afraid to love wholeheartedly. My mother was a funny, warm-hearted, nonjudgmental woman. She raised me to be kind, patient, and understanding. It's through both her nurturing and my suffering that I can relate to most people I encounter.

Even though I am stronger for it, at times I'm still the broken little girl on the floor that needs her mommy. I feel I need her more now, in my thirties, than I did back then. Who is going to answer the unanswerable questions in my life? I guess it just means I'll need to work harder to find answers myself. I'm up to this. After all, we Motherless Daughters become quite self-sufficient. It's a beautiful thing.

Phoebe,

thirty-four, whose mother died in an accident fourteen years ago

My mother was killed by a drunk driver when she was forty-nine years old. My brother, age thirteen at the time, was with her and was nearly killed but survived with no long-term *physical* problems. My parents had been married nearly twenty-two years. I had been living away from home for about three years and was married with a fourteen-month-old baby boy.

I was very close to my mother. We talked nearly every day and saw each other weekly (we lived a little over an hour apart). My father, on the other hand, was very emotionally distant and withholding. Nothing was ever good enough for him. He had a short temper but was not what you would call physically abusive. He was in the military for more than twenty years, so we moved quite a bit while I was growing up.

I honestly couldn't tell you how I've gotten through life to this point with my sanity intact with everything that happened concerning my mother's death and the chain of events I believe it spawned. What basically happened after my mother died is as follows: I got involved with an old boyfriend; I was divorced from my first husband; got pregnant with my second child by the old boyfriend; lost custody of my son to my first husband's mother, who lives in another state; moved back home with my father; had another baby boy; not long after my son was born, married someone I barely knew who was physically and mentally abusive; and divorced after a year. I moved back in with my dad and started school, moved in with a man I met there and then married him within a year, finished school, got a good job but quit after three years to move to the Virgin Islands when my husband got a job transfer, and lost everything I owned in Hurricane Hugo; my husband had an affair (he still lives with the woman now). My father died from prostate cancer, leaving all his money to the National Wildlife Federation (money from the lawsuit related to my mother's death, part of which my brother and I were supposed to have received in the first place).

At about that time, I moved back to the United States; went back to my old job; lost more than sixty pounds in less than three months and started a borderline eating disorder; divorced again; was involved with an abusive, crazy man; got pregnant and had an abortion; got away from him; and lost one of my best friends, my "almost second mother" who took me in after my father died and helped me get back on my feet in the States. After dating many, many men, I finally met the most perfect person for me, someone who is very good to me and whom I love and respect more than anyone. Now I'm happy, but I still miss and need my mother. I still think of her every day.

I was able to type out this nice, long list of events, which doesn't give any weight to their significance, but they were all major, life-altering events that severely disrupted my life. I feel like I was caught in some kind of whirlwind, completely out of control.

I am not proud of these events, most of which I brought on myself. It hasn't been until the past couple of years that I realized a lot of this had to do with my mother's death. What bothers me the most, and what I hesitate to tell people for fear of what they'll think of me, is the serial marriages and relationships and, most importantly, losing custody of my son. I'm considered an intelligent, stable, mature, dependable, responsible person who is not difficult to get along with and not the type of person to have had all this happen to. It seems to me that all this boils down to having an emotionally distant father and to losing my mother so young. These two things have created such an emptiness I was always trying to fill through relationships and pain I was always trying to numb. All my marriages occurred within a five-year period following my mother's death—by the time I was twenty-three, I had been married three times.

My brother is even worse off. As a teenager, he got involved with drugs and alcohol and dropped out of school. My father sent him to a residential drug rehab center when he was fifteen or sixteen and told him, if he ever used drugs again, he would be kicked out of the house. He was kicked out the next year and has been on his own ever since, living with me a couple of times. Just after the "accident" he told me that he felt it was his fault because he had talked my mother into staying at his karate studio, where they were on their way home from. No one in the family ever blamed him or said it was his fault, but he denies having said this now. He goes from menial job to menial job, place to place, and person to person. He has always had a drinking problem and has had some DUIs—even with his mother having been killed by a drunk driver and himself almost killed! I have tried to help him on more than one occasion, but he only takes advantage of me and lies and steals from me. Although we live in the same city, I never hear from him unless he wants something. He has learned that I won't loan him money anymore, so I don't hear from him very often. My son adores him, and we feel like he's the only family we have now, but we don't really have him at all.

My son never knew his grandmother and is saddened by this. He loves for me to tell him stories about her, and he seems to love this woman he has never known. I had a horrible adolescence, and my mother and I were just beginning the adult phase of our relationship. I felt as if I had almost "made up" to her for all the trouble and pain I had caused her, and then she was taken away from me. There is still so much I would like to know, talks I'd like to have, things to share and do together. At the same time, I'm glad she didn't have to grow old and ill or suffer from a long and painful illness, and I'm glad she wasn't around to see my father go through his illness or to have to live without him after his death.

I am definitely independent and extremely strong and resilient. People often tell me they are amazed that I have been through so much and not only am alive and sane but also am a very optimistic, upbeat person. I have not allowed any of the bad experiences in my life to make me bitter or bring me down. I have always ended up better off after each adversity. At the same time, I still feel like a scared little girl who needs to be loved and taken care of. I don't want to be a martyr and hope I don't come across sounding like one. I only want people to understand and to accept and love me as I am. I believe I've found that person, but I have such a high regard for him that I feel "flawed" and as if I have to constantly explain everything so I'll feel he'll understand. This all comes from me; he doesn't do anything to make me feel this way. Men in the past have said they felt as if they couldn't live up to my high standards and expectations.

Sometimes I fear dying in a car accident or some other tragic way, but I also fear not knowing what diseases I may be predisposed to. I don't know if my mother would have acquired breast cancer, some other form of cancer, heart disease, or any other number of diseases. She had smoked since she was a teenager and never wanted to quit. Actually, now I'm kind of glad she didn't, because, as it turns out, it wasn't necessary for her health. Her older sister, however, did die of lung cancer two years after my mother's death. Yet I still smoke! I know it's stupid, and I always thought it was because I was highly addicted and just didn't want to quit. I wonder now if it isn't part of "risk taking" or a feeling that I'm going to die some tragic death at a young age, so there's no need to quit. Or perhaps I'm just testing the limits of my own mortality.

One thing I've done to stay close to my mother and to find out more about her is genealogy research. Several years after her death I began researching my extended family history on my mother's side. I didn't grow up around my extended family, and I barely even knew my grandparents. I work on this research to this day.

Betty,

thirty-nine, whose mother died of cancer thirteen years ago

My mother died when she was just fifty-three years old. She had cancer (three types of leukemia, including a childhood type). Her pain from the disease was misdiagnosed as a "sprained leg" by an indifferent doctor. What she had was phlebitis *with* the leukemias. She entered the hospital for chemo five months before she died.

She was a valiant fighter. She used to tell me that even though she felt the doctors used her like a guinea pig (she had five rounds of different chemotherapies in less than six months' time), she hoped what she suffered would help someone else live.

Unfortunately, because of his own emotional dysfunction, my father made the choice to leave my mother in the hospital to die, even though Mum wanted to be at home. I was in my late twenties—the oldest of five children, all born within seven years' span—and refused to believe that my father's unilateral decision was the final word. My younger sister, my then-husband, and I set up a meeting with the hospital doctor to discuss the practicality of letting my mother go home. When the doctor walked in and discovered that my father was not part of the meeting, he refused to talk with us and walked out of the room.

My mother died sometime after Johnny Carson's monologue (she rarely missed his opening monologue), all alone, in reverse isolation in the oncology ward. Those are still bitter memories.

I've been through the grief stages and through counseling, but the times I will miss my mother the most are, I know, yet to come.

My first husband was abusive. My mother knew, at least as much as I dared let anyone know at that time. We divorced about five years ago. Now I am a newlywed, wanting a family, wanting my wonderful new husband to know my mother, wanting her to know him, wanting my mother to be Grandma to my children . . . the list never seems to end. I want my mother to rejoice with me in my new life and love, but . . . she's not here.

I, too, have experienced the unthinking cruelty in the remarks of those who have mothers and just do *not* understand. I know the sick feeling and little-girl shame that sometimes comes from the well-meaning, cheery "encouragement" to get on with my life or the reminder that it's been "years since she died" (unspoken: Why does it still bother you?).

I think another factor in my grief and pain was that my father never dealt with his loss. He immediately began to date the mother of my brother's then-fiancée. (He hardly knew her and pushed my mother for an introduction.) In less than five months after my mother died, my brother's engagement broke off, and, instead, my father married the ex-fiancée's mother. It's hard to grieve healthily when your mother's place is already "filled."

Subsequent losses hurt so much more now that my mother is no longer here. I am glad we became good friends before her illness and death, but then there are all those shared moments that are now missed. No matter who the other person is, it's not the same as a moment with Mum.

Lauren,

thirty-seven, whose mother died of heart disease fourteen years ago

I'm the mother of a six-year-old son and in the process of getting a divorce. My mother died when I was twenty-three, of an unexpected, degenerative heart disease at age fifty-four.

I was very close to her. She was my biggest supporter and fan. We really enjoyed each other, staying up late into the night talking, smoking cigarettes, and drinking water. We read the same books, and she was intelligent and open minded.

For a number of years, probably ten, I just couldn't deal with her death. In my family, we never even mentioned her name for years because it upset my dad so much. Because it hurt too much to feel, I just numbed out that part of me. I tried to compensate by compulsive overeating and smoking (until three years ago), getting overinvolved in other people's lives trying to re-create that security, and mothering others.

Perhaps my mother's death elevated what her importance in my life was to be. If she were alive, she may not have been that big of an influence, but the loss of her prevents me from knowing that for sure. To me, she was my biggest supporter and I lost that. I lost that person who thought I was the greatest, no matter what.

I know if my mother were alive we would fight, she would make me mad, shame me—the usual irritating things mothers do. She would also love me, listen to me, support me emotionally, cook for me, care for me, mother me. I could have somewhere to go home to where I didn't always have to be in charge and "on." I still miss my mom with tears in my eyes when I let myself think about her.

Liesl,

thirty-eight, whose mother died of cancer sixteen years ago

I was almost twenty-three when my mother died. She was fifty-eight. Like you, I was just beginning my journey as an adult. And also like you, I often have a sense of "being stuck" at that stage of my development, that I've not emotionally matured past twenty-three years of age.

How has the loss of my mother at a young age impacted my growth? How could I have come so successfully into adulthood in spite of it? I have everything and more than she had wished for me: a career; a loving, happy family of my own; good friends. Still, there is a vacant place within my soul that I persist in maintaining for her. It is sixteen years later, and she is still missed at the Thanksgiving table. She was missed at my daughter's birth, first words, first steps. She is the person I want to phone after my husband and I have had a tiff. But I think her absence is felt most at ordinary moments, like when I'm shopping for baby clothes, tending my garden, driving down a beautiful stretch of road—and listening to my friends "complain" about their own, still-living mothers. So many times I want to chide others for the way they take their mothers for granted. And just as often, I feel real envy for their ability to pick up the phone and share a chat with Mom.

Only a few days after my mother died, I dialed her number just to hear it ring, to fantasize she was out of the house on an errand. In a way, I think I am still doing this mentally and probably will continue. It's my way of keeping her alive, and of keeping her with me.

Robbie,

twenty-three, whose mother died of cancer eighteen years ago

I am the youngest child in a family of six children, five girls and one boy. My mother died when I was five years old of cancer that began in her throat and spread way too quickly throughout her body. She was a beautiful, gentle woman who died seven months before her forty-second birthday. My sisters were nineteen, sixteen, thirteen, and eight years old. I am still grieving over my mother, and I feel as though it is a process I will be going through for the rest of my life.

One of the most difficult aspects for me is that I have no recollection of any of the five years prior to my mother's death, or the next two to three years after, and then I can remember only bits and pieces. I wonder if that time will ever come back to me at all in some form or if it is completely lost in some mental repression chasm that I cannot quite reach. I have always thought my sisters were lucky because they remember Mom, whereas I can't really remember her at all. Yet I miss her so much. I can't tell you how many times I've thought, *If only she were here, this wouldn't be happening.* Some days I miss her so very much that I ache and I can't stop the tears.

I have a theory that some people think is a little strange, so I usually don't tell anyone, but I wanted to share it with you. I wonder if other motherless daughters do this as well. When I pray, I pray to my mother as well as to God. The reason for this is because I honestly feel as though my mother is my guardian angel. Throughout my life I have been in many situations that were bad for me or life threatening, from having unprotected sex when I was younger with chances of pregnancy and diseases like AIDS to car accidents to police situations. Yet I have been fortunate in that I have always come through okay. Despite being in such situations, I am all right and my life is the way it should be, at least according to me. Even when something bad has happened, I feel it is my mom trying to teach me a lesson somehow, to turn me in another direction before it gets worse. Maybe because she wasn't able to stay in my world long enough to teach and tell me some things herself, this is how she compensates.

I was lucky that I had the rest of my family. I consider myself raised by my father and my sisters, who all gave me very much love and caring. My father remarried a year after my mother's death, and my sisters really had a hard time with that. None of them really have a good relationship with my stepmother, who had two children of her own, making us eight. She doesn't help the situation either. She resents all of us a great deal, probably because we are living proof that my father actually loved someone else and had a life before her. I know she has had a hard time with me simply because I look just like my mother, and according to everyone in my family who knew her, even have her personality. My father tells me that God took her but left him me. I don't take this negatively, though. As a matter of fact, I take this as a very special compliment.

Marie,

forty-six, whose mother died of a stroke nineteen years ago

My mom had just turned fifty when she died. She had recently lost a lot of weight and, after years of taking care of everyone else, she was finally having some fun. Then the phone call came. We huddled in hospital waiting rooms all weekend as she fought to come back from a vicious stroke. Finally the doctors said her fight was over. Release forms were signed, and we huddled around her hospital bed, hoping she could hear us tell her how much she'd be missed.

Then she was gone. And I was a motherless daughter.

A week after we buried her, my elderly neighbor caught me as I was walking out to get the mail. "I heard about your loss. I'm so sorry. I lost my mom forty-two years ago and I still miss her every day." I appreciated her condolences, but the thought of living with that suffocating grief for the rest of my life honestly scared me.

I was holding back tears during the day as I mothered our two toddlers, waiting until they were asleep in bed before I allowed myself to hover in the shower, weeping into my hands, for as long as the hot water would last. I craved a place where I could go scream at the top of my lungs, "It's not fair!"

As much as he wanted to help, my husband felt lost too, not knowing what to say. I cried myself to sleep every night, telling him I felt like I'd been pushed over a huge cliff, into an adulthood with no backup. The thought of my mother not being there as I navigated the rest of my life was too hard to comprehend.

Weeks passed. Then months. The first anniversary of my mom's death arrived, and I couldn't believe I'd lived a whole year without talking to her or hugging her. My babies had a whole year of developmental changes she would never know about. I still had dreams where we'd dig up her grave and it turned out she was still alive and thankful we'd come to save her. It still wasn't real that she was gone.

I'd learned about the "stages of grief" in college, and the "acceptance" part made me furious. It would never be okay that my mother died. I'd never be able to accept it.

After she died the hub of our family was gone. We gathered that Thanksgiving and ate the first turkey my dad had ever cooked and talked about how much we all missed her. But soon we stopped gathering. My dad was moving on, setting up his new life, and my siblings and I kept in touch individually. We no longer felt like a team. But if it weren't for that, I don't know if my husband would have taken the job that required a move to the East Coast. We've lived in five amazing states since then, and it helped his career immensely.

I was born with a deformed foot, and my mother was deeply entwined in the surgeries I had as a child to correct it. She'd always felt like it was her fault I'd been born with it at all. Nine years ago I made a huge decision: to have my foot cut off. I finally decided that I wanted to start over. Because

I had the surgery, I now live a pretty active life with my new bionic foot. I know she'd be happy to see that, but the irony is, I don't know if I could have done the surgery if she were still alive. It would have bothered her deeply to know I wanted to cut it off.

A song came out around the time of her death that has lyrics close to what I'd imagine she would have said to us if she'd had a chance to say good-bye. It talks about hoping that life treats us kindly, wishing us joy and happiness, but above all wishing us love. On my daughter's thirteenth birthday, the child who is named after my mom, I was driving home after a mother-daughter night out, looking over at her as she told me what she liked about the movie we'd seen, and a sadness fell over me. I was sad that my mom couldn't see what an amazing young woman her namesake had turned out to be. Then that song came on the radio. Tears flowed down my face.

Another time, I was leaning over my mother-in-law's shoulder as she flipped through pictures of our family's latest adventures, and suddenly I had a twinge of sorrow that I'd never show this set of pictures to my own mom. At that moment, the song came on the radio behind me. This song has come on the radio at too many perfect times for it to be a coincidence. I strongly feel it's my mother's way of telling me she's still here, watching over me.

Would I rather have her here, physically? Yes. But time has moved on and life has unfolded without her. This is the reality I live with. I continue to raise my kids and count my blessings that my dad found a wonderful woman to be their step-grandmother. I have visions of what my mom would have been like now, with these teenage grandchildren. My husband tells me I've grieved for the idea of what life should have been like, and I think he's right. I was mad that she was gone, but I was also so very sad that the life I'd imagined was not going to happen.

Now I feel like I'm waiting for the day that I hear about a young neighbor losing her mother so I can be the older woman, there to tell her that I lost my own mom forty-two years ago. And that it's okay to still miss her. Every single day.

CHAPTER FIVE

Lives Shaped by Loss: Twenty Years and Beyond

Having lived through two decades or more since the deaths of their mothers, the daughters in this chapter show evidence of even deeper levels of reflection and awareness. They've had ample time not only to think about the long-term effects of mother loss but also to see how that early event will influence the course of their lives. Their stories are longer and more richly developed, more retrospectives than letters.

Because so much time has passed since each death, these daughters often find themselves surprised by the intensity of the grief that still bubbles up from time to time. Subsequent losses in particular, such as a father's death or the loss of a job, can send a daughter back to mourn another piece of her earlier loss and may trigger the same emotions and fears she had when her mother died. It's important for these women to remember that mourning can only be resolved *to the best of a daughter's ability at any particular time in her life*. That's why the daughter who feels she's worked through her grief for her mother at age thirty, for example, may find herself facing additional challenges at thirty-eight that send her back to rework the loss from a more mature and experienced perspective.

By now, a significant transformation has typically occurred: the daughter's longing for *her* mother, who continues to recede further into the past, has often been replaced by the more generalized longing to be mothered. When we use the word "mother," we're not always referring to a specific person but often to a set of behaviors we associate with a maternal figure: security, support, comfort, nurturing. Adult motherless women haven't lost the need or the desire for such a figure in their lives. By their thirties and forties, however, many have become aware of their tendency to project this need onto other relationships. Forty-seven-year-old Madelyn writes that her first marriage failed, she believes, in part because she expected her husband to make up for the familial love she lost when her mother died. Thirty-three-year-old Joanne writes of her caution when enjoying intimacy with her young daughter, for fear that she will try to extract the love from her daughter that she imagines she'd get from a mother.

Several daughters in this chapter are approaching or have already reached the "magic number," the age a mother was when she died. Unlike most of their peers, who must live into their seventies or eighties to exceed their mothers' final ages, most women who lost their mothers young reach this transitional time in middle age. In her book *How to Go On Living When Someone You Love Dies*, psychologist Therese Rando calls this kind of threshold a "correspondence phenomenon." Reaching the corresponding time in one's own life often causes increased anxiety and sudden upsurges in grief, she explains. Motherless women who are approaching the magic number often feel a powerful urge to live a full life, with no excuses and no regrets. Explains forty-year-old Laura, whose mother died twenty years ago at the age of fifty-four:

> I live with the fear that my life will be cut short, as my mother's was. I have the desire to cram in as much as I can before reaching age fifty—the year of my mother's cancer diagnosis and mastectomy. So what do I do? Scuba dive, sky dive, white-water raft, ski, travel. . . . People think that I have a death wish. They just don't understand that if I don't meet certain challenges now, there might not be enough time to experience the thrill of these activities *later*.

Reaching the magic number can be a time of both sadness and rebirth. The daughter fears leaving her mother behind—and may feel guilty for seeing years her mother never got to see—but also feels relief that her destiny will differ from her mother's. Forty-year-old Gayle, whose mother died at the age of thirty-six, says her thirty-seventh birthday was "spooky." All day long, she recalls, she kept hearing the *Twilight Zone* theme song playing in her head.

Women who have children often find themselves having a similar response when their first child reaches the age they were when their mothers died—a second significant correspondence event for motherless daughters. For the first time they understand, as adults, how much a child of that age knows and feels, and they can see how much that child still needs a mother.

By the twenty-year point, a daughter's mourning for her mother involves continually contextualizing the loss, assigning it—and reassigning it, when necessary—a meaningful and appropriate place within her larger life story. A death becomes easier to accept when its perceived outcomes include public benefit and personal growth. Forty-five-year-old Ilene writes about how the absence of a strong female model has given her the freedom to choose her own path. Seventy-eight-year-old Kate tells her story to classrooms of women to help them create and understand their own personal narratives. Other daughters write of enjoying particularly close relationships with their children, deliberately choosing nurturing partners, and devoting themselves to professions that help others cope with loss.

Yet despite these personal achievements, periodic feelings of loneliness, insecurity, and longing remain inescapable. Our early experiences are the building blocks of the self, forming the foundation for the women we become. When I began sorting through the letters for this chapter, I expected to read only stories of personal victory, as if the insight a motherless woman gains over the decades inevitably translates into a sort of wisdom and peace unique to her. Although it's true that the daughters who appear in this chapter seem to have achieved a deeper level of acceptance regarding their losses, we must not confuse acceptance with resignation. What we see in this chapter is a bouquet of women who have learned they can change the present and the future, but not the past. The focus in their letters has shifted away from mother loss and toward the long-term effects the death or absence has had on daughters who weren't allowed to grieve and who were subjected to a family's secrecy, betrayal, or neglect.

As these daughters lead us through the stories of their lives, they show us how the circumstances that precede and follow a mother's death can be, over time, even more difficult to reconcile than the loss itself. Daughters who do not receive good substitute mothering and do not have the opportunity to express their feelings and mourn may become what psychiatrist Vamik Volkan, the author of *Life After Loss*, calls "perennial mourners." They're always longing, always hoping, always searching for the idealized mother figure who will erase their troubles and help them feel whole.

As I've traveled throughout the world for the past twenty years speaking about mother loss and the long-term effects of early bereavement, I have tried to stress one point whenever possible: how essential it is to support young daughters—and sons—*at the time of loss*. According to a recent national survey sponsored by Comfort Zone Camp, a bereavement program for children, 11 percent of Americans will lose a parent before turning twenty. To address this need, hospitals and hospices need more health-care professionals trained to work with families in crisis; local bereavement programs need empathetic volunteers; and bereaved children need consistent, ongoing emotional support from relatives, teachers, family friends, and neighbors.

The same Comfort Zone survey also revealed that 72 percent of the adults who lost parents before age twenty believed their lives would have been "much better" if their parents hadn't died so young. Together we must keep working toward an open, honest approach to early parent death so that girls who lose their mothers today will look back in twenty years and tell us more stories of triumph, of being compassionately guided from a place of confusion and pain into territory that one day also includes gratitude and growth.

* * *

Laura,

forty, whose mother died of breast cancer twenty years ago

Twenty years after my mother's death, I still have her seal coat in my closet. Sure, I've thought about restyling it through the years but just never got around to it. I guess subconsciously it was comforting to know that a part of my mother was close by. I think it's about time that someone a bit more needy should benefit from its warmth.

My mother died at age fifty-four from breast cancer. I was twenty years old (three weeks shy of my twenty-first birthday) and just two weeks away from returning to college to complete my senior year. I not only lost my mother, I lost my best friend. As an only child as well as a fatherless daughter (my father died when I was one and a half years old from a heart attack), I grew up always knowing I was a little different from my peers. My mother chose never to remarry because she did not want anyone else raising her child. All of her energies went into providing for me as best she could.

My mother instilled a sense of independence in me from day one. Given her situation, a widow and mother in the early fifties, I doubt anyone would have questioned her parenting had she swung toward overprotective behavior. She did not, and for that I will be eternally grateful.

What has kept me on course these past twenty years since my mother's death has been (1) a very loving and supportive family who has never held back tears when discussing the impact of her loss, (2) a core group of friends who either knew my mother or who were sensitive enough to ask me about her, and (3) a deep inner drive from within to enjoy life and succeed— a fitting way to honor her memory!

Until recently, I felt that I had worked through just about all there was to work through as it related to mourning for my mother. I was wrong. Something happened to me during a self-defense course. We were asked to develop a "custom conversation scenario" whereby we would have the class "mugger" represent our worst nightmare, be it realistic or symbolic. The idea is that unless we free up the opponent within, we will otherwise ensure failure.

I had the mugger represent cancer. For the first time since my mother's death I yelled and screamed at the disease. I was able to verbalize at a very loud pitch, in the company of a very supportive staff and fellow course members, just how destructive the disease had been. The scenario ended up with me knocking out the disease (the mugger) before it consumed me. I had no idea just how much emotion had been churning within me. What a catharsis!

I still fear the onset of cancer, but I'm starting to view age fifty-four differently—not as an ending, but perhaps as a new beginning.

Gina,

thirty-five, whose mother died of breast cancer twenty-two years ago

My mother died after a two-year bout with breast cancer at the age of forty-two. As I read your story, I was angry that practically ten years later the disease still had the same characteristics, taking women like your mother in two years at the same age as mine.

I had just turned thirteen two weeks before my mother passed away. Although much of that time is now a blur of emotions and isolated events, I do remember feeling so out of it. Connected and not connected. Confused. I was the oldest; my two sisters and brother were eleven, seven, and eight years old, respectively.

My dad, whom I consider a truly incredible man, vowed to raise four young children on his own. And he did. When I think back, though, growing up was incredibly difficult. I remember thinking, *This wouldn't be such a problem if Mommy were around.* Whether it was makeup, clothes, or boys, I felt like I was sailing in completely new seas where the captain of the ship was as clueless as I was. My dad did the very best he could, which by most standards today, even for children who have two parents, was damn good. Still, there were gaps and holes and confusion. Your book helped me be able to start looking at those areas and not feel as if I am betraying my father. I can't be angry at a man whose love and devotion were always so obvious, but I can be angry that there were areas he could not fill in, through no fault of his own.

Today I am thirty-five years old and very single. Although I long to be married and to have children, I just haven't seemed to have the luck. Recently, I started looking around at all my friends who are married and having families, and comparing their lives to mine. Why do they seem to be entitled, while that part of happiness still eludes me? I know it was no mere accident that my mother's three daughters are still single (ages thirty to thirty-five), while her son is very happily married. And I know it probably has to do with my early loss. My sense of independence, my desire to achieve all that my mother hadn't in her lifetime, my fear of loss and of being left, my incredibly tough standards for men . . . all have contributed to my situation as a single woman. How to change that still confounds me. But I feel that maybe now I know where the problem lies.

After many years of searching for a place for myself, I am now a middle school teacher. I live three thousand miles away from my roots and my dad, sisters, and brother. In the four years I have been teaching, I have had contact with children whose mothers died during their middle school years. This year, a student with whom I had developed a very close rapport lost her mother to lung cancer. Unlike my reactions to other students' losses, my reaction to Jennifer's loss was incredibly intense. I wanted so much to be there and to help and guide, and yet I was even more upset because of all the things I know lie ahead for this very dynamic young girl. I can't help with those things. I also know what strength and independence and determination she will develop; I see it happening already.

She came back to school two days after her mom died, in an effort (I think) to capture some normalcy and get some attention for her grief. That morning, she and I spent a few hours walking around campus talking and sharing experiences. Not only do I think and hope it helped her, but I know it helped me to give something back to the world. When my mother passed away, it was one of my seventh grade teachers who, with just a smile and a hug, provided some much-needed comfort. All of this makes me wonder if there are truly any "accidents" in my life. . . .

When I moved away from my family almost eight years ago, I was finally able to deal with a lot of the grief. Before that, I felt that if I dealt with my grief openly, I would somehow add to my family's. I just couldn't make things more difficult for my dad (who remained single all these years) or for my siblings. Three thousand miles away, I gave myself permission to grieve. The mourning comes in waves, depending on what major event or age I am passing through. I have been in and out of therapy and know this will probably be a lifelong process.

Rosemary,

thirty-six, whose mother died of asthma and heart failure twenty-three
years ago

I don't think I fully understood the impact of my loss for fourteen years. When I was twenty-seven, I was diagnosed with
breast cancer. While I was in the hospital after a lumpectomy,
I had a bad reaction to the anesthesia, and my release date was
delayed. I was in my room alone when a woman appeared. She
said she had heard I wasn't feeling well and wanted to come
see me. She looked at me and said, "You look like a motherless
child." I was stunned, because at the moment I realized I was
one. It didn't matter that my dad had been great (and had
even waltzed me around the hospital corridor the night before the surgery) or that my family and friends had been very
supportive. I realized that I needed that maternal warmth surrounding me. My visitor held me and we talked about faith—
her from a black Baptist perspective, and me from a Jewish/
Taoist/New Agey one. We spoke for maybe fifteen minutes
and then she left. By the next day, I was well enough to go
home. I sought her out and found her in bed. It seems she
had had a mastectomy the day before she came to help me out
and was feeling the effects of it that day. I was very proud to
sit with her among her family and hold her hand and tell her
how much she meant to me. Even now, almost ten years later,
I am grateful for her presence in my life.

I think, perhaps, it is the experience of finding myself
alone, without a guide through the labyrinth of a woman's

life, that is the essence of being a motherless daughter to me. I have many women friends ranging from contemporaries to women in their fifties and friends of the family in their seventies, but knowing what it would have been like for my own mother might have helped me face life differently. I am now contacting friends of my parents and getting their perspective on my mom. It's interesting to find that twenty-three years later I have become someone much like her. I love hearing about her generosity and fearlessness, but equally important is hearing about her insecurities, which somehow make my own more understandable. I appreciate finding her in me and finding the parts of me that are unique to me.

I find I miss my mother the most when life changes occur, such as when I see my body aging and as I watch all my friends getting married and when I turned thirty. I also miss her when life feels a bit overwhelming and I wish I didn't *need* to be so self-sufficient. Much of the time I don't consciously "miss" her, but there are times when I would just love to sit down to tea and cookies and just talk—about anything and everything.

Janet,

thirty-six, whose mother died in a private plane crash twenty-four
years ago

My mother died when I was twelve years old. Because she
died an accidental death and my father (who died eleven
months before her) died from heart disease, my father is the
one whose death gives me the most personal worry. But my
mother's death served to crystallize my awareness of death.
She was very good to have around when my father died, and
she managed to squelch any fears or worries I harbored because of his death. Unfortunately, that meant when she died
I was totally defenseless and unprepared, as if I had never lost
a parent.

That is when the nightmares started, and I began thinking about death pretty much all the time. I am hyperaware
that death can come at any time, to anyone, which makes me
careful to notice life and enjoy it. Unfortunately, it also makes
me unnecessarily morbid, and I'm constantly preparing for
the unexpected, which is a waste of time. My mother's death
made me superstitious about the sorts of things that make
people "knock wood"; I tend to try very hard not to offend
"them" (whoever causes things to happen). This gives my husband no end of amusement, in a kind way, and his reaction
helps keep me from going overboard.

Not having a mother since I was twelve has meant that
I missed a lot of the basics. Sometimes that's not so bad. I'm
a terrible ironer, so my husband does it all, and I'm a lousy

housekeeper, which is fine because life's too short to bother rearranging dust. Sometimes, though, I'm keenly aware of things my mother would have taught me that I didn't work out on my own until my thirties: simple social customs that everyone knows but me—reciprocal invitations, hostess manners, etc., that can be interpreted as rudeness instead of ignorance.

My mother was a very strong woman, very opinionated, outgoing, and demonstrative. She was involved in everything, mostly for our benefit. (When I told her I didn't want to be a career Girl Scout like my older sister, she heaved a sigh and said she could finally quit the Girl Scout Council.) I was young enough when she died that I still thought she was the voice of right on everything, and I never questioned her opinions. To this day I'll notice that some silly belief I've had all my life is one of her ideas, and it's totally fallacious. Some were obvious and discarded when I was still in my teens (such as "redheads can't wear pink"), and some I just jettisoned last week ("babies shouldn't be picked up every time they cry"). If she were still alive, we'd probably be going around and around about most everything, because heredity or environment has given me her spirit. I'm just as opinionated and outgoing, although, I believe, more tolerant. I am a confident woman, which I believe is her gift to me. She supported me and bolstered me and helped me build a tremendous amount of self-esteem in the twelve years I spent with her. Very few people can get me down or bend me to their will, but I know for a fact that if she were alive, she would be able to push my buttons with deadly accuracy. I don't know if she would, but I know she definitely could.

My mother-in-law has always considered me less—less socially acceptable, less mannered, less like regular people. I think I was the first orphan she knew, and I had to be, by definition, a charity case. She couldn't relate to someone who spoke her own mind, lived her own life, knew where she was going and what she wanted. Instead of recognizing that as a personality type, she blamed my motherless condition. In her opinion, my mother would have taught me how to hold my peace, to knuckle under for appearance's sake, to speak and move like a "lady," and to never tell anyone how I really felt. That's the way people work in her family. Lucky for her, she never met my mother. I've often watched as my mother squared off with her in my fantasies. My engagement, college summers, my wedding: my mother would have minced her in moments, not in the pointed, articulate way I would have hoped for, but in her own bulldozer way, the same way she mowed down all the people who treated any of her children unfairly or cruelly.

My mother has been dead nearly twenty-five years. Her death has made me independent, caused me to take responsibility for myself, and allowed me to make my own choices. But I still miss her almost every day. I still feel some anger toward her for dying and guilt for the anger I showed her the day she died. She's never met my terrific husband or my beautiful son. She's never here when I need to be folded up in her arms. When I cry for my parents, it's my mother I want. When I need a person like me, someone who's honest and direct, she isn't here. She's not on the end of a phone line. She's nowhere.

Lindsay,

forty-eight, whose mother died of accidental carbon monoxide poisoning twenty-four years ago

In the middle of December 1988, the earth stopped spinning. Everything in my life is measured before and after that day.

On that day I was a mom to a chubby, delectable, nine-month-old baby girl. My husband came into the kitchen with the mail and there were two cards from my mom: a first Christmas card for the baby and one for my husband and me. I read the cards and showed the baby the one from her grandma.

Then the phone rang. My younger sister was crying and sort of blurted out that Mom was dead. I doubled over. "What do you mean?" She explained that it looked like Mom had died of accidental carbon monoxide poisoning. I couldn't breathe. My brain would not compute. I was clutching the cards in my hand. "You're wrong! I just read her cards. They just came in today's mail! *No!*"

The circumstances were just freaky enough to make the front page of the newspapers. And it was on the news. I watched a "teaser" for the 6:00 news that showed my mother's body in a body bag, being taken from the RV where she died. I saw this alongside my twelve-year-old brother. What do you say when you see something so startling? I told him I was sorry and felt a level of shame deeper than I have ever known. Nice people don't see their Mom in a body bag on TV.

My folks had just divorced after twenty-four years of marriage. It was a relationship fraught with abuse, physical and mental. She was finally free, except now she wasn't. And my dad went berserk. There were threats against us kids, people removing guns from his house. The police became involved, trying to calm things down.

My heart broke again, and again I dealt with all the arrangements as the oldest child. My mother-in-law and baby traveled back home with me. My baby saved my life. Her eyes were my mom's. Her smiles saw past my pain and into the future. Smelling her, feeling her skin. Watching her suck her thumb. She is the reason I didn't walk off a bridge and into the river that runs through our city.

Over the next year it was my daughter, again and again, who kept me alive. I wanted so badly to give up. But everyone reminded me to look at her when I felt that way. My husband showed great compassion and willed me to keep going. How he kept the faith, I'll never know.

I became pregnant that year. I kept thinking the new life in me would bring my mother back in some way. But it wasn't meant to be. Less than two weeks before the anniversary of my mother's death we learned that our baby had died inside me. The guttural wail that came out of me was for the baby and my mom. How was it even possible? This is when I became clinically depressed. *No shit*, I wanted to say.

For almost seven years afterwards I couldn't hear Christmas carols without becoming physically ill. Going into a retail store after Halloween brought panic attacks if I heard them on the overhead speaker.

My daughter, and three years later, her younger brother, kept me focused. I was still experiencing panic attacks and depression, but now I had a therapist and meds for the anxiety. And I *wanted* to keep going. I finally realized that, as upset as I was, I wanted to live, to love my husband and babies, and to see my kids grow up.

I had work that I loved and it kept me involved in life, too. Between my sweet little family, my work, and the love of family and friends, I put one foot in front of the other. My sister and I became close in a way we had never been before. It's like we made a pact: Motherless Sisters, Unite.

I had a reading by a gifted "seer" a few years ago. My daughter was going off to college, and I was experiencing the loss of my mom all over again. The seer told me that my mother's presence was strongest when my daughter and I were together. That Mom was watching over us. Before the reading she didn't know my mother was gone, but she was right. I see and feel my mom a thousand times in my daughter.

This year my niece got married—the first grandchild to marry. I put together glass lockets for my niece, my sister, my daughter, and me. It had a photo of my mom on one side and my grandmother on the other. We tied one onto my niece's bouquet with a lovely Tiffany blue grosgrain ribbon so that they were there with us in a tangible way.

I know there will be more milestones that my mom is not present for. Sometimes it pisses me off. Sometimes it makes me sad. And sometimes I know that she is here and fully present, in a way that she could not have been if she were still on earth.

I will always be wounded. I know that she wouldn't like that. She would want me to be free—she was a free spirit at her core. But I am not. I will have the anxiety and, from time to time, the depression as reminders that the price to be as free as I am now has been high. So I will just have to walk on, knowing that it's okay to miss her and love her. I have such moments of hurt twenty five years on, but I also have moments of sheer joy, mostly in the form of my daughter and son. Something they say or do is her, utterly her, and I am soothed. I feel like I could stay in those moments forever. But still the wound, while expertly covered, is deep and wide and real.

Joanne,

thirty-three, whose mother died of alcoholism twenty-four years ago

My mother died when I was nine years old, and, at nearly thirty-four years of age, I agree it changes everything. My family cannot seem to speak about my mother in any realistic way. My father only describes her as a warm and "glowing" woman who loved her babies. Her father can speak of her childhood now without too much pain, but her adult life is a mystery to me.

My mother lost a baby boy to spina bifida when I was four years old and was told by a doctor at that time that his death was her fault. I feel that this is when my mother truly died. She was able to be a mother to her children before this incident, but afterwards she was only attempting to stop the pain of living. As a result, I know very little of my mother. My older brother remembers her loving certain nursery rhymes and singing him to sleep. I only remember her drinking.

I have found many photos of her that are so strikingly like myself—in physical ways, like gestures and postures—that they seem eerie. At times I feel as if I'm a photocopy or a ghost of who she must have been at one time. A counselor once told me that she must have been quite a special person to have affected so many people so deeply. But no one is able to speak of who she was or what she was like.

The special bond between mother and child existed between us even through the alcoholism. Her kindness remained, and she seemed to be a person dying of some strange cancer rather than from drink.

When she died, it was as if all that I had trusted was ripped out of my life. Now, as a mother myself, I find that at times I hold back. I love my daughter fiercely, but I find a sense of sadness in that, as if it makes me more vulnerable to future pain. My attempts at relationships are always a search for the mother that died. I am constantly reminded that I have no one I can go to when I need to be held. I wonder at times if the feelings I have when holding my daughter are different from other women who hold their daughters, women who don't need extra love from their daughters because they have a source in a living mother. I try to assess every relationship and gesture on my part to see if I am expecting too much or hoping for too much in the way of a deep connection between hearts.

What you say is true: losing a mother was not "meant" to happen. It strengthens us and gives us character, but I for one am tired of being strong. I'd give it all up for being wrapped in her scent and her hug.

Gayle,

forty, whose mother died of cancer twenty-seven years ago

I recently underwent treatment with a psychiatrist, and I found that the "hole" I was carrying around with me, that space that only a mother can fill, had become large enough to begin interfering with my life.

I just turned forty-one the other day, have a good marriage of seventeen years, one child, and a normal, basic life. I work in a good government job and have never been abused or had any real problems in my life. The two most significant events of my life were my mother's death in the winter of my thirteenth year and my son's diagnosis of diabetes when he was ten months old. The two events were major sources of grief, as you can imagine, but I dealt with my son's diabetes much better than I did with the death of my mom. I was an adult at the time of my son's diagnosis, and you're right: children don't know how to grieve. I still think of myself at the breathless, expectant age of thirteen, and I know I was still very much a child. My point in telling you all of this is to let you see that I am in every other way "normal" (whatever that is), with a happy childhood behind me and a pretty good mainstream life now.

After starting therapy, I realized I needed it some time ago. My sister, who was seven when Mother died, didn't remember much about Mom, so as the years passed I found myself being her memory of Mom. We also have a brother who is four years younger than me. When my sister finally married at the age of thirty-four, I found myself cast in a slightly different role than before. Suddenly my little sister didn't seem to need me like she used to. I was unaccountably depressed that summer, although I put on quite a happy face.

I had always felt that after twenty-seven years I shouldn't feel so sad near the anniversary of Mom's death, that I shouldn't feel so empty at the thought of her being gone. But I did. Mostly the pain was muted in my everyday life, but as my son has gotten older and I have told him about her, it's returned. She died of cancer, and I remember everything that happened in the six months she was ill as if it were yesterday. When my son asked innocently if she died of AIDS, what should have been a humorous question was like a knife splitting open a ripe fruit full of grief. I knew I needed help.

I have always had a weight problem, and through therapy I realize that I started stuffing myself with food after my mother's death. I stole money from girls' purses for years after that and hoarded food. I was convinced that whatever was good in my life wouldn't last, that I had to get what I needed on the sly. My father did his best with three kids and asked my maternal grandmother to live with us to help out. She did so and gave of herself selflessly for four years (a fact she reminds us of, when it's convenient). In an effort to keep things as normal as possible, they didn't show us their grief much, and we continued our school and life activities as before. Only recently have I learned that my father paced the house at night, unable to sleep, and often came home from work early, too broken up to remain at the office. I never knew those things, and I now hurt for him. In their kind but misguided attempt to hide their pain, the message I got was that my grief was somehow too volatile and scary to let out. I *needed* to let it out, but I somehow felt it was undignified and had to remain unexpressed. Consequently, it remained and it surprises me every now and then with its sharpness and intensity.

My mom was thirty-six when she died, and the day I turned thirty-seven was one of the oddest days of my life. My mother actually died four days after turning thirty-six, but the reality of living longer than her didn't hit me until I turned thirty-seven. It was a Sunday, and I was puzzled by my lack of enthusiasm that day. I hadn't started examining and making peace with my inner feelings of loss yet, so they were still a mystery and a source of self-recrimination to me. After some years of unfulfilling employment, I had been working in a terrific, challenging job for about two years at that time and was enjoying professional success. My personal and family life were in good shape; I was overweight but happy in every other area. But I found myself not counting my blessings that day, and I couldn't figure out why.

I looked at my then-ten-year-old son and was overwhelmed by the urge to sob—what would happen to him if I, like my mother, died at this age? He was a loving child and so full of promise and excitement about life. The thought of not seeing him grow to manhood was physically painful. It literally sucked my breath away. I looked at my husband and imagined how lost he would be if I died, and another knife pierced my heart. I found myself mourning the imagined loss of our future together, the plans we'd made, the dreams we'd had, and it felt so real it was frightening. It was like being in a slow-motion train wreck—inevitable and unavoidable—and I couldn't get off. Where the heck did this come from? Instead of being happy for having lived thirty-seven years and contentedly planning for the future, I found myself mired in these morbid thoughts of unreal loss. I felt so guilty about my feelings, I didn't share them with anyone else at the time— keep those dirty little negative outlooks to myself, can't embarrass myself by letting them out.

Perhaps the weirdest occurrence (and funniest, as I look back on it now) was that the *Twilight Zone* theme song kept running through my head all day. I couldn't shake it, and I still don't know what fertile minefield it emerged from. I spent the day absolutely baffled by the power of my grief, rather than celebrating my life. I now know that I was grieving for the losses my mother suffered as she died—including her loss of her future. How awful and terrifying that must have been for her. The sad little thirteen-year-old who lost her mother all those years ago was trying to get out and work through her feelings of loss, too. It took me another couple of years to identify those feelings, and I'm just now feeling okay about feeling lousy about the loss of my mom. I now find myself wondering what Mom would have done with her life after we three kids grew up and left.

I can see now that my need to hide my grief led me to hide other aspects of my life as well. Consequently, I am a closet eater and I buy excessively when things are on sale. Sounds trivial, but I can see the connection, and it's not a healthy response to a sale, believe me. If I couldn't ask openly for something I needed, I'd get it in any way I could—thus the stealing. I remember taking small pleasure in the sympathetic reactions of a couple of friends, including my first boyfriend, shortly after Mom's death. Instead of being comforting, it was yet another source of guilt. What kind of person *enjoys* the attention paid to her because of her mother's death? A quite normal, confused adolescent girl, it turns out.

I married well, to a stable man who is just now understanding some of the things I've wrestled with in private for twenty-seven years and openly only for the last two. All the mother stuff has come out in therapy, although I've always suspected it was there. I still make bad food choices, but this year when the sad fog that accompanies the anniversary of Mom's death surrounded me, I relaxed and let it come. For the first time ever the tears I shed were cleansing and somehow comforting. After twenty-seven years, it was okay to feel lousy about losing a mother I adored and relied on. After all these years, I finally thought of that pain as something other than bad and inappropriate. This time it was an identifiable thing, and although it wasn't exactly welcome, I let it wash over me and just felt bad about it for a couple of days. It felt good to acknowledge it without guilt. It felt good to just feel bad. Is this healing? It's too soon for me to tell, but I hope so.

Although my life has not been pathetic because my mom died, her death did affect me in ways I'm just now beginning to understand. I was always a can-do, by-the-bootstraps kind of woman. I think I got that strength mostly because I had to get along after Mom was gone. And that's good. But I was also judgmental: Why couldn't others manage their lives like I did through adversity? I'm softening, learning to accept weaknesses in others, as I'm learning to accept the damaged parts of me.

Abby,

forty-two, whose mother died of breast cancer thirty-two years ago

I was ten years old when my mother died. I was her firstborn of three daughters, and we had always been very close. It was not the first death I faced in my childhood, nor was it the last. Before I was twenty years old, I saw the passing of an uncle, two aunts, and both grandmothers. My mother and two of her sisters all died of cancer in their forties, leaving behind a total of seven daughters (spread across three families) and two sons. We, in some ways, form the basis for a small, controlled study of our own. One surviving aunt stepped in and took on the first set of cousins whose mother died. Those cousins have led the most emotionally stable lives among the three families. However, when their aunt/stepmother died recently at the age of eighty, they insisted upon referring to her as their mother at the funeral. This puzzled me, because it seemed a denial of their birth mother. It was almost as if they wanted to prove that their lives were more normal than they actually were. The other two families have struggled much more obviously and outwardly with our mothers' deaths and the changes that resulted. In my case, there never was a stepmother, but in the other family of cousins there was a quick remarriage to a woman who was extremely different from the rest of our family.

The year my mom died, I was invited to take her place beside my dad at a family gathering for parents only. I'm sure no one realized what a powerful burden that placed upon my eleven-year-old shoulders. I would say that my mother's death ties for first place as the major influence upon my life. The other one is my relationship with my father.

An aunt once remarked that something in my father died with my mother. I think she was right. For years he was very fragile emotionally, and I remember the scary feeling that he might snap suddenly without warning, but counseling was not an option he chose for himself or for any of us—although I have subsequently chosen it during several difficult periods of my adult life. Instead, he carried his pain deep within. On rare occasions he would burst into tears when he mentioned her name, or his unusually calm temperament would transform into a rage out of proportion to our behavior. All of this was disconcerting to me.

As the second of four brothers, my father knew little about raising daughters. He also knew very little about running a household. He hired a series of live-in housekeepers, all of whom we resented greatly. The first was a woman named Mrs. Roberts, with a big German shepherd. Only the dog was allowed to come into our house through the front door. Mrs. Roberts threw all of our toys away while we were at my aunt's house for the week after the funeral, and when we returned all of the neighborhood children had mysteriously acquired our toys on garbage day. Our next housekeeper had a young daughter who fought viciously with my sisters and slandered my father when he tried to intercede. It went on and on.

Within a couple of years my sister and I had taken over all of the household chores—shopping, cooking, cleaning, washing. It was far better than either my father's attempts or the parade of unloving women who invaded our home. We became highly competent homemakers, always reminding our father to sit back and let *us* take care of things. We saw him as far less than competent at domestics, and for good reason. An old friend of mine still remembers my father sponging up a table spill with his shaving brush. He also washed his dinner dishes in the bathroom sink so that he could dump table scraps down the toilet to avoid clogging the sink drain. The bathroom he knew about, but the kitchen he didn't. Engineering, romping around with us on the carpet, and bedtime stories were his area of expertise. Hugs and intimate conversation and all the subtleties of mothering were foreign territory. I grew up feeling responsible for my father's and my sisters' well-being, yet many of my own basic needs were not being met. This took its toll on me in later years.

I grew up feeling highly competent but insecure, outwardly silly but inwardly serious, extremely mature for my age but completely naive about certain basic social skills. I frequently felt on the fringe of social groups. My sisters and I shared an intense relationship that combined parenting each other with the usual antics of sibling games and rivalry. I saw myself always as somehow more gifted than most children because I had insight into the importance of life and health. I took long walks alone on the beach and wrote deep poetry. I had the feeling a death was hovering around the corner. At one point I even had a formula for how frequently a death in our extended family would occur. On the outside there was joy and laughter and strength. On the inside was sadness, fear, and vulnerability.

Although I had lots of flirtations, I didn't have a steady relationship until I was twenty-one. It was a healthy relationship in many ways, yet I couldn't move beyond a point in terms of commitment. This relationship lingered for years, even after we moved to separate towns and began seeing others. Then I fell into a long-standing pattern of entering relationships that were going nowhere in the long run.

It took my father's death when I was thirty-four to really snap me into completing the grief process. Several weeks before my father's sudden death from a long-term illness for which he had never been hospitalized, I collapsed at a party after a few sips of wine. I woke up in a state of constant panic, from which I did not emerge until months after my father's death. I had lived hundreds of miles from home for years and had traveled extensively on my own, and I was not particularly the greatest at keeping in touch with my dad, but I believe that the deep psychic bond between us was pulled as his death approached, causing my physical and emotional reactions. Though neither of us was totally conscious of it, we had formed a powerful connection that went beyond words and miles. Even the doctors who tested me after the bizarre sequence of physical events confirmed this belief, citing numerous similar examples they had seen in their careers.

My father's death triggered the grief process that had not been completed after my mother's death twenty-four years earlier, even though I had worked on it in counseling and journaling for years. It suddenly hit me so strongly that I wanted a life of my own beyond my connection to my parents and that I needed to let out all the pain of the past in order to have this. Although I had not been one to shed many tears in the past, I now cried for hours each day. I was so distraught that I had to stop working for a number of months. Much of the year following my father's death was spent grieving the loss of my mother.

At the end of that year I felt a renewed sense of self. I moved in with my sister and returned to graduate school. My sister and I supported each other through the grieving we had left to do. I received a departmental award when I completed my master's degree. At the end of the year I moved into an apartment of my own and began teaching at a couple of colleges in a nearby city. Within a couple of months I met the man who is now my husband.

I married late, at age forty. I have never had children, though I now have two wonderful stepsons. I have always felt ambivalent about having my own children. But I feel that I am coming into a new sense of self, looking for other ways to be a creative and fulfilled person. This growth is, in part, spurred on as I approach the age my mother was at the time of her death, forty-four. I want to envision possibilities for myself that she never knew. And the closer I get to her age, the clearer it becomes to me that we each were given our own paths to walk in life. Believing in this gives me huge amounts of freedom and joy.

Denise,

forty-two, whose mother died of acute myeloid leukemia thirty-two
years ago

My story of mother loss begins when I was four and my mom was tired, tired and bruising easily. I can picture being thigh-level with her, and seeing these magnificent, swirling purple, gold, blue, red, and sickly green splashes decorating her legs as she did the dishes in her yellow polyester self-sewn shorts. She didn't remember how any of the bruises happened.

It was May 1976. After a brutal testing regimen, including barbaric bone marrow samples, my mom was diagnosed with acute myeloid leukemia. She spent three months in the hospital over that summer, leaving me in the care of my father and older siblings. I ate ice cream cones and root beer barrel hard candies purchased from Mother Hubbard's Cupboard in the mall by a string of relatives who visited from far away, and I missed my mom.

Her immune system was weak, and I was a kid who played in the dirt baking masterful mud pies. When I was allowed to visit her, I was covered head to toe in too-big hospital gowns, booties, gloves, hat, mask, then instructed to stand just inside the door. My beautiful, salt-of-the-earth mother appeared wan, but her face would light up and she would wave me over and pat her bed for me to hop up. I would dash, tripping on my oversized costume, straight to her arms, worrying the whole way that I would make her sicker and she wouldn't come home again.

When she died in 1981, my mother was forty-three. I was nine. My brothers were twenty-one and nearly nineteen; my sister, fourteen; and my dad, a widower at age forty-five. We were all too young.

Somehow, we had to keep on living. My dad showed initial promise, despite the death of his wife of twenty-two years, but he chose instead to marry again nineteen months later. This woman came with her own set of baggage overflowing with mental illness, addiction, and misguided expectations. We call the years they were married "the Dark Ages." I was neglected emotionally as my dad and his wife tuned out and drank up. I muddled through high school and dropped out of college after spending that first year missing most of my classes because I was listening to "dead mom songs" by artists like U2 and Madonna. I rewound my cassette tapes over and over and over, feeling the sadness, loss, rage, and abandonment in each lyric. I howled through this pain that I had never let myself feel before. I reached out to my sister, and we began forging a deep relationship that we both needed to navigate our twenties without a beacon to whom we could return.

Revisiting my grief has become cyclical, usually spurred by milestones that I experience without my mom. When I was twenty-five, I packed up my hatchback and putted across the northern Plains, over the Rockies, and down into the Great Basin, where I planted tentative roots in the unforgiving caliche of the Mojave. I never expected to stay.

However, on my first day of work at my first job in my new town, I stumbled across the man who would become my husband. We didn't date right away but became friends instead. After much cajoling, I let him into my heart. Then I lay in his arms, vulnerable and sobbing. I cried for hours because I knew I was feeling the truest love, love like I hadn't felt since my mom rubbed my back as I fell asleep each night. I cried because he would never know her. I cried grief-filled tears because, after nearly twenty years, finally, I was safe. The wedding we planned was unconventional because our family situations were unconventional, so we married in a ceremony attended by strangers as we stood on the rocky shore of Oahu, with only my mom's spirit in witness. But I still missed her.

As I rode the waves of marriage, I wanted to know my mom as a woman and not just as a mother. I wanted to know her hopes and dreams. I wanted to know how she loved my dad, why she loved my dad, how she could ignore his idiosyncrasies. And I wanted to know how she felt as she tried to have babies. My own journey to motherhood, though not nearly as excruciating as some, was far from smooth. I knew that my mom had miscarried several times and had lost two infant children. I couldn't talk through any of this with her.

From those around me, I didn't feel I would find the patience I thought my mother would have had to listen to me work through my fears and frustrations—not just over my fertility but also my worries that I couldn't possibly be mother enough. My mom had her hands in everything creative: calligraphy, bread making, knitting and crocheting, designing and sewing, writing, playing piano, growing an abundant garden that reaped gallons of produce for canning and baking and feeding her family, neighbors, and friends—all while offering up her veins to chemotherapy injections. How would I make my hands as worthy of holding an infant and raising a child?

At age thirty-two, I held my moments-old daughter in my tentatively maternal hands. I was amazed by this human being that had appeared, and I felt my mother's love wash over me. As my husband and sister slept nearby, I held my girl and looked into her alert eyes sparkling in the low lamplight, and I told her all about my mom, the angel, who was watching over us at that moment, who loved us more than any other. The two of us huddled together in the middle of that night, and I prayed I would be enough.

By age thirty-four, when I held my newborn son, I was angry. I was angry that my beautiful mother wasn't there to be a grandmother for my children. I was angry that I didn't have her help. I was angry with my father for checking out so many years ago. How could he deny the love a parent feels for their children? How could he have shed his responsibilities so easily? I grieved what could have been, what should have been.

Now, I am forty-two and my daughter is nine—spookily close to mirroring the ages of my mother and me at the time of her death. I know the numbers don't really mean anything, but I can't help feeling like I am learning something from this similarity. It's a reinforcement that I am not my mother and my daughter is not me and we are not destined to the same fate. Cycling through the steps of grief has become less of a surprise to me by this point. Each time that I thought I was "okay" with my mom's passing, I would endure another round of processing her absence. It would come up again when my father died and my sister and I fell into a heartbreaking estrangement that following year.

Revisiting my grief from time to time can feel like a step back, but I find my way two steps forward. Along the way, I've found friends who each help fill in the gap left by my mom's death. Especially helpful during the past seven years of my journey has been the Daughters Without Mothers group that meets once a month in my town. Through this group, I've found three kindred spirits whom I will always know and love and count as family, as well as many other women who have touched me, heart and soul, as they bared theirs. Through our "dead moms" group, I've found trust and empathy, a place for dry humor and wet, wet tears. I've found women who "get it" and make no bones about my continued exploration of grief and living without my mom.

I have a close relative who once suggested I've made a career of my mother loss. That stung, especially because it came from my mom's only sister. I know what she was trying to tell me, but on the other hand, I cherish that I don't have to apologize for still missing my mother the first Thursday of every month when I gather with a handful of motherless daughters to share our stories.

Jill,

forty-six, whose mother died of breast cancer thirty-four years ago

Twelve years old is a challenging time in a girl's life. You're no longer a kid but you're not a teenager, and as hormones kick in the body changes. Life can be confusing and a little dramatic. My twelfth year started this way. I am the youngest of five, and my three sisters were close to or in adulthood, so it was my brother and me at home. Our father was a minister, and we were considered lower middle class, never enough money to really have our needs met but always encouraged to have faith that someday things would get better. I knew my mom was sick but it was never directly spoken about. Frankly, I felt that if I knew it to be true, it would mean she was dying. So I chose to not know and nobody ever sat me down to talk about it. I learned to tune out my instincts and see things from the perspective of "if I don't acknowledge it, then it doesn't exist."

I was taking an interest in boys and played my Leif Garrett album repeatedly on our hi-fi. I had acne, thick glasses, and a gap between my two front teeth. I wore a bra because all the other girls had them, not because I needed one. I dreamed of going to California and becoming an actress. I wanted to be someone but I wasn't sure if I wanted to be me. My dad was often working and sometimes that included travel. My mom was sleeping a lot and seemed easily annoyed. Sometimes I could hear her sobbing in her bedroom. I didn't know how to comfort her and I felt upset that dad was always so busy.

I saw pictures and had heard the stories, of how my mom had been a model in Manhattan when she met dad. She even knew Greta Garbo. Dad was fresh out of seminary and proposed to her on their second date. They married in 1951 with a beautiful ceremony. The black and white photos still look so glamorous. My dad was an intellectual and an incredible speaker. He was always supporting positive change in the world and stood alongside with others against social injustice.

I remember my parents sitting together in the backyard, drinking martinis. They laughed and flirted with each other, but things seemed to change dramatically when mom became sick. That year when I was twelve, I saw her becoming thinner and sadder. It seemed as though everything was hanging by a thread.

I needed my mom to help me understand who I was and to reassure me that I was normal and smart and pretty, yet I felt guilty to be so needy because I wanted my mom to live. I was afraid that I could deplete her of the energy she needed to get stronger, so I tried to be as quiet as I could be. I felt as though if I stopped praying or stopped trying to make myself invisible that mom would die.

And then dad died instead. He had a massive heart attack. He was fifty-one.

Five months later, mom died. Breast cancer. She was fifty-three.

I was twelve.

People say time heals all wounds. To a certain extent I think that's true. The grieving process can carry one through to a place of acceptance. It's more complicated when you are still dependent on the person who dies. I was sent to live with relatives a thousand miles away who I barely even knew. My needs were met in the sense that I had a roof over my head, food to eat, clothes to wear, and a school to go to. But there was no affection, no discussion about feelings, no reassurance or direction. I was often told I was a "survivor" and that I would be a strong person because of this.

The most confusing emotions came at times like high school graduation when I felt proud of myself, but the deafening silence when no one was there for me left me feeling devastated. So much so that I didn't even attend my graduation from college. While planning my wedding, I found myself at one of the happiest times of my life feeling suddenly swallowed up in a wave of depression because I wanted to share picking out dresses and flowers with my mother. The same thing happened during my pregnancy.

When my marriage ended, it was necessary for me to go back and look at patterns throughout my life. I now understand how things went in a direction that didn't make sense to me at the time. I've been very blessed to still have my best friend from age twelve. Her parents embrace me as an unofficial member of the family. But the voids can never really be filled.

Because of my loss, I have a very clear understanding of the fragility of life and limits on time. I truly do try to stay aware of the present moment and appreciate each day. What has come as such a pleasant surprise is the mirroring back, the reassurance that I craved so desperately from my mother before and after she died, has gently surfaced with my precious five-year-old in ways I never expected. I can see in how she is growing and developing her sense of character and her sense of self that there is a reflection that speaks to me and quietly says, *you're okay, you're on track,* or *pay attention,* and that has been extraordinarily healing for me. My sensitivity to it has made me a better parent despite my lack of reflection with my own mother.

Melinda,

forty-six, whose mother died of complications from systemic scleroderma thirty-five years ago

I remember the last day I saw my mother alive. I was eleven years old, and it was just a few days after Christmas. Dad had packed her an overnight bag to take her to the hospital. It was an event I had grown accustomed to over the past year, so, giving her a hug, I said goodbye, and ran outside to play. Almost thirty-six years later, the regrets of not having said more to her or done more for her still haunt me.

My mom developed systemic scleroderma over the course of about two years, and at the end of her life at age thirty-five, the disease had weakened her internal organs to the point she developed pneumonia. By Christmas she had grown too weak to sit up, so we decided to move our family—all thirteen of us—into the small bedroom at my grandparents' house for our traditional gift exchange. There was a different and strange atmosphere in the room that day, as if my father and the rest of my aunts and uncles knew some horrible secret but were trying to keep it from me.

My father had to work to keep our bills paid, so it was largely up to me to help take care of Momma in her last months. That meant helping her take baths, rubbing lotion on her dry and blistering skin, holding her fork at dinner because her hands and fingers had "petrified," and doing my best to listen and understand when she lashed out in pain, fear, or sheer frustration at her rapidly increasing immobility. There are still times I feel that there must have been something more I could have done to lessen her pain or to have helped give her one more day here. It was a tremendous amount of responsibility for an eleven-year-old girl to handle. But I loved my mother and would do anything for her. I also loved my father, and I didn't want to see him suffer or leave me like Momma did. So I grew up fast.

Although my father quickly remarried—less than ten months after my mother's passing—I still felt a tremendous need to protect and take care of him. I never saw him cry at Momma's funeral, and the thought of it happening was something I couldn't bear. So I spent many years of my life "taking care" of my father by not speaking of my mother.

There are many events that I often wish my mother had been here to witness: my first period, making All-County Band in the eighth grade, getting my braces put on and removed, high school graduation, college graduation, surviving a hysterectomy, and meeting my husband.

Throughout my adult life, I ventured to numerous counseling sessions to come to terms with the emotions that I had learned to keep inside with little or no success. During my previous marriage, I attempted to begin working through Momma's death and purchased a copy of *Motherless Daughters*. Upon seeing it on my nightstand, the response from my husband was that I "was living with too many ghosts." That was it. No support. No encouragement for such a brave step. I put away the book and continued my journey silently. That was ten years ago. He is no longer in my life. I'm sure Momma is pleased about that.

Two years ago, my current husband came home with a book that had been recommended by a counselor. He had been reading the first few pages and was very excited about it because it really helped him to better understand how I was handling my mother's death. He showed me the book—*Motherless Daughters*. I smiled, told him my story of the "first attempt" at reading it, and we started reading it together.

Do I miss my mother? Most definitely. Do I feel that I am who I am today because of her death? In part, I do. Do I feel that I could have prevented her death? No. But I do believe that I can honor her by helping others who lost their mothers at a young age to find their voice in the grief process. To tell them that it is okay to be sad, that it is okay to be afraid, that it is okay to be angry. But most importantly, to know they are never alone in this.

Madelyn,
forty-seven, whose mother died in a fire forty years ago

My mother died in a fire that destroyed our home when I was seven years old. My father and my six-year-old brother and I survived. I was burned much worse than they were and spent about a year in the hospital. I have scars on my body still. Strangely enough, even though I have these scars, I have been called beautiful, striking, and attractive for reasons I have never really understood myself.

I have few memories of my mother, but when I think of her, I remember that it was she who came to my room and wrapped me in a sheet and carried me down a burning staircase and handed me to my father, who put me out on the front lawn with my brother. I have heard people say that she returned to the house, perhaps to save something. I remember that I cried to my father when he went into the house after her, "Don't go—Mother's gone."

My father and brother went to live in my aunt and uncle's house, and I joined them when I got out of the hospital. I had a nurse for a while, but I don't remember much about her. After she left, my cousin Trudi came to live with us, also at Aunt and Uncle's. I suppose she was in her twenties then, and she was to look after us. Trudi was the best thing that could have happened to us except for Aunt and Uncle. Or, rather, all of them made possible for us as normal a life as possible under the circumstances.

I don't remember too much of my father during that time, although I know from pictures I have of us that he read to us and took us to the country during that period. He had another house built, and after about two years we moved— me, my brother, Trudi, and Daddy. I guess our life was normal. Most every memory I have of that time is of the beach, Brownies and Boy Scouts, and trips Trudi took us on. She was strict but fun—we did not feel unloved.

I remember very well the day my father took us to visit a woman at her parents' house. I also remember one night in the den when he told us he was considering getting married— and I said, "We want you to be happy, Daddy."

We were told Trudi was leaving to go home, and my brother and I were sent to summer camp for three weeks. When we came home, Gloria, our new stepmother, was there. We were nine and ten years old then. I guess we assumed life would go on as normal, with just a "new" Trudi. Instead, it was the beginning of a special kind of hell: my grandmother was not allowed to visit us at our house; most of the time when we got home from school, Gloria would be in her room with her mother visiting her; one day in her car, Gloria told me we should be nicer to our father because he didn't have to keep us.

Gloria was and is a very cold person. Now, as an adult, I can say she was a vicious, jealous, greedy creature.

She left my brother alone, mostly. However, it seems I could do nothing right, and I began to be punished physically, mostly by being slapped in the face.

At some point my father began to start the same treatment toward me. Once I spoke up and said something about Gloria not being fair, and my father slapped me repeatedly, time after time with both hands until finally I started screaming. I remember him stopping and saying to himself, "What have I done?" over and over.

As I got older, this changed somewhat. First my father took my brother and me aside one Sunday morning and told us we were adopted but that only meant we were really wanted. Then, later, Gloria and Daddy told us Gloria was going to have a baby.

After their son was born, Gloria mostly left us alone, but we weren't allowed around our half brother at all. Our bedrooms were upstairs, and Gloria had an extra room turned into a den. That is where my brother and I spent most of our time. We got plates and ate upstairs alone most of the time.

One strange thing happened that I have never forgotten. My father accosted me one morning demanding to know what I had been doing. It seems some "serviceman" had written me a letter. I was about fourteen then and frankly was a tomboy. Almost every free moment of my life was spent at the stable with horses. I didn't know any serviceman or even anyone outside our town. I asked to see the letter, and Father said Gloria had destroyed it. My father was accusing me of something I didn't even have an understanding of. I believe, and always will, that my stepmother made this up or created the scene.

It was strange—being afraid and angry and helpless, yet even at that age I was outraged at the injustice. Finally, in the eleventh grade I was sent away to school, and then I went to college and then to work and then to marriage and then to divorce and then to the real work world. I hardly ever saw Gloria or Daddy once I went away to school. They had another son and built another house.

On my honeymoon, my father called me and asked if I told my husband what a bad father he was. I loved my husband, but I drove him away, I believe, with the hidden anger and impossible requirement that he make up for the love I never had. This is my biggest regret.

Once, after I divorced, I visited my father's office to store some papers there. In a file marked "Family Corresp." I saw a letter he had written to business associates when I was in college in another state. It said he would appreciate them checking on me because I had "problems" but that it was not necessary that they have me in their homes.

It was then, I believe, that I let go of my father—not let go of the past, but let go of hope—and although he died in 1989, I think that as my "daddy" he died then for me, when I saw a man so weak he would use the reputation of a child to cover up the sickness of his wife.

My brother and I have been close off and on, but he has a family and lives in another state now. The last time I saw him was at Father's funeral. Neither he nor I were mentioned in his will, and although we did not expect to inherit anything, it was strange not to have ever heard from his executor. It wasn't an emotional feeling, really, just more like feeling. Isn't it odd how people can change a life or hurt a life just by wishing you away?

Now I am forty-seven. I have decided that love is loyalty and true concern for another's quality of life and well-being. I have done some good for some people—I have probably hurt some—I could have been worse—but then I could have been happier.

If it seems this is not about Mother, it is. One thing I have thought about for all these years is the day a woman came to interview me because Gloria was to adopt us formally. To her questions I said yes or whatever I was supposed to say, because I was afraid. But what I wanted to say was, *No, no, no.* I had to get a new birth certificate for a trip, and when I saw Gloria's name listed as my mother, I felt sick.

I am having a hard enough time as it is making a living, but every week I think as soon as I can afford the legal fees I am going to find a way to undo that adoption, if it is the last thing I ever do.

At my father's funeral, after everyone left, I slid a snapshot of my mother into the crack of the lid of his coffin—for the man he was when he was with her, and for her.

Someone asked me recently if I get lonely, and I said to myself, "So what? I've been lonely all my life." Even if I had not gone through the abuse from my stepmother, I think I would still have that corner of lonely, maybe not so big but still there. My mother loved us; she saved me. But there was no time for her to see me become a person and love me, good or bad, right or wrong, always. A mother is always there for you, and if you have enough time for memories, she is always with you, even when she is gone.

My cousin Trudi, who knew we were adopted, asked me once if I was curious about who my real parents were. Perhaps I am not normal to not wonder or not care.

I had a real mother. My mother. Her name was Rose. She died in a fire after saving her children when I was seven years old.

Simone,

forty-four, whose mother died of accidental electrocution forty-three years ago

Today marks my forty-fourth birthday, but it is my forty-third birthday without my mom. I was there when she died but I don't remember it. I was only thirteen months old.

All my memories of my mom belong to someone else. I don't remember her or know anything about her firsthand. All I know about my mom is through stories, like a legend. I yearned to know about her but was often afraid to ask questions for fear of upsetting others or feeling sad. Even into my thirties, it felt strange to talk about her. It almost felt taboo.

In grade school I would draw pictures of Mom, trying to guess what she looked like. What color was her hair? Her eyes? Most family photos were in black and white, so it was hard to tell. In some of my drawings, she wore wings and flew with the angels.

It's hard being motherless. Most kids don't understand why you come to school with tangled hair, crumbs on your face, or rumpled clothes on dress-up day. Some kids were cruel and teased that my mom died because I had ugly red hair. Because I didn't have a mom to tell me otherwise, I started to believe them.

Occasionally I fantasized that Dad was lying to me. Mom wasn't dead and was going to come home someday. They had a bad fight but she was still coming back. Maybe that blond lady in the grocery store was really my mom—following me to ensure I was okay. But, then again, maybe the kids in first grade were right?

The truth was hard to take. When we lived in Thailand, Mom was electrocuted by a metal fan in our apartment when we were home together. A neighbor heard my nonstop crying and called the apartment manager; I often wonder how much time had passed. It's strange how a child's mind works: when others would ask how my mom died, I would say she was taking a bath and a fan fell into the tub. I don't know where this story came from; I guess it made more sense. I really believed the bathtub version until about eight years ago.

Mother's Day was *not* a celebration. In school the teachers made us make a Mother's Day card. I remember meekly asking the teacher whom I should make a card for because I didn't have a mom. Nervously, she suggested that I make a card for my dad or grandma. This was puzzling. Didn't she know that dad would get a card on Father's Day?

Dad remarried when I was twelve. I now had a mom, but I didn't know what I was supposed to do. She didn't really act like I thought my mom would act—was that okay? We both tried but it wasn't easy for either of us.

My dad used to tell me that my mom loved me very much, but I had no context, no ruler, no beaker to measure how much love filled her heart. That is, until I had my daughter. Shortly after her birth, I started to understand the capacity for a mother's love. Mom really had loved me! She didn't want to leave me. The birth of my daughter released so many new emotions, so many feelings, questions, and so many unknowns. There were so many things I needed to ask her! I had been motherless for all the rights of passage: scraped knees, puberty, dating, first kiss, prom, graduation, wedding, pregnancy, and childbirth. I thought I should be over "this mom thing" but I soon realized my journey had really only just begun.

At the age of thirty-three, I realized that I had never had the chance to grieve the loss of my mom. I knew that it sucked not having a mom, but because I never really knew her, I didn't know just how much I was missing. Then I learned about Motherless Daughters (MD) groups. I couldn't find one in my city so I started my own. It was the best gift I've ever given myself. I found a safe place to share my tears, frustrations, realizations, love, and joy with the other courageous women who were ready to share their stories. We share a bond that (fortunately) few understand. Through this sisterhood, it has been easier to talk with my dad and my kids about my mom.

My son was born two days after my birthday. When he was thirteen months old, I was the same age as my mom when she died, and my son was the same age as I was when she died. Unintentionally, I did the math and was irrationally nervous at the anniversary of her death that year. Would I live to see his second birthday? Would something happen to me so that I wouldn't be around to raise my amazing kids? When I shared this with my MD sisters, they understood.

At our meetings we strive to honor our moms: we share stories, pictures, favorite possessions, and even recipes to facilitate healing. To outsiders, our conversations may sound cold and sarcastic, but for us they are therapeutic. Women who are new to the group often ask if it gets any easier. We've come to the conclusion that not having a mom doesn't get easier as time passes. The pain dulls a bit but doesn't go away. It simply is different. As I have shared my story, at times I think it was better to lose my mom so young because I didn't have to live through the immediate grief and don't have memories, like the sound of her voice or the smell of her perfume to miss. However, my MD sisters who lost their moms when they were older can't imagine not having any memories of their moms. They savor the good memories and lament the bad.

Ultimately, we decided that there is no good age to lose your mom. It's rough no matter how old or well-adjusted you might be. In the end, we honor our moms by not dwelling on the past, taking it a day at a time, and caring for ourselves and loved ones.

Fran,

sixty-two, whose mother committed suicide fifty-nine years ago

I was born into a family of Italian immigrants, and my mother committed suicide when I was three. There is so much to this story that I have even written a novel, hiding myself in 1855 Italy to try to attach some meaning to my feelings.

My mother's death was a scar on my Italian Catholic family. I was not told she committed suicide until I was about thirty-five, by my sister who was ten years older when I needed to know the cause of my mother's death for medical reasons. Her life and her death had become the family secret. If I asked, I was told not to ask silly questions. My father moved into a hotel and referred to my mother only as a Madonna. I was placed with my maternal grandmother. My sister was placed in an all-girls Catholic school, where I had little contact with her until she was married. She died a very, very difficult death at fifty-five of obesity. I feel her story should have been heard, but she learned early not to ask or tell.

I was not told my mother had died until about six months after her death. Instead, I was told she had gone away. Not even any angels or heaven! I reacted by running to the train station and streetcars, waiting for her to come home. Not until I was about fifty-eight did I demand some answers, but still very little was given to me.

I bore the guilt; it was my fault. I had been very ill with ear infections and had a mastoid performed on me. The doctor cut my facial nerve, leaving the left side of my face paralyzed. As young as I was, I have memories of my mother crying, trying to make me pretty again, sitting on the edge of the bathtub as she curled my hair. My grandmother would tell me I was a pretty girl if I did not smile.

I felt I never belonged, as if I was simply a boarder and that when I grew up, I was expected to leave. I lived with my sixty-five-year-old grandmother, my sister when her husband went overseas during the war; and then, when my mother's perfect sister remarried a wealthy man when I was twelve, I moved in with her . . . but again it was not my home. At one time, as a small child, I fantasized that I would change my name to "I Love You" just so I could hear those words spoken.

All my financial needs were met—none of the emotional. I, too, was sent to Catholic school. What a great substitute for a mother—nuns! I learned to survive by being the good little girl, never letting anyone close to me, and becoming determined that I would grow up and marry a handsome, ambitious man and have four children. I would become the mother that I did not have.

I did marry and have four children. I was often frustrated being a mother, for there was no pattern for me to follow as a mother or a wife. With God on my side, I am very proud to say I have four great children and five perfect grandchildren.

The marriage ended in divorce after thirty-four years. He was first-generation German born, workaholic, alcoholic. That is another story. I entered therapy to deal with the divorce and my anger. I realized that the divorce had very little to do with my anger and the real issue was my family of origin. My mother didn't think me worthwhile and copped out of life. My father chose not to be in my life to fill any emotional needs. My grandmother was too busy cleaning and crying because my grandfather had a series of mistresses. My maternal aunt, very good at providing all the material things I needed, was busy cultivating her role in society. There was no time for me, and I knew that I could not ask.

I did therapy in the Gestalt method and the visualization method, and went to workshops and anything that could help me break through this idea I had that I was not good enough, pretty enough, thin enough, smart enough.

I do believe that somehow my mother still is with me— not in spirit, because I did not know her, but in the children I have borne and the children they have borne. I see actions and hand movements that I don't recognize, and sometimes I think to myself that maybe, just maybe, that look or that action comes from my mother and she somehow lives.

I am what I am because of my life, because of what I have been and done. I still have an issue with trust, but I no longer fear abandonment. I walked through that and I survived. I write. I paint. I am happy with my creativity. I live well, travel, and all in all have learned to love myself as much as I have expected others to love me. But I still wonder, what if?

My mother chose not to live. I have resolved this. The distorted lies that my family chose to tell me have been the most difficult issue to resolve.

I survived at the time, and that was enough. Now I live because of the life I have created. My wish is that for all motherless daughters.

Kate,

seventy-eight, whose mother died two hours after her birth

I received your book on my seventy-eighth birthday as a gift from a young friend. I quickly scanned it for references to women who lost their mothers at birth, that tragic time of "her life or mine." I started reading and kept right on through to the end, with epiphanies along the way. Losing a mother certainly makes a difference in how a life goes.

My mother bled to death about two hours after I was born. She was seventeen. When I was just past two, my father remarried a woman who had no use for me. I stayed with my maternal grandparents, aunts, uncles, and extended family in a small village of about three hundred, surrounded by cattle ranches.

Today, I tell my life story over and over to women of many different cultures—Polynesian, Asian, Caucasian, and that unique culture of army wives. I started teaching a class called "Women in Transition," and the responses I get from the women indicate that I have been effective in making my story universal.

I had a childhood memory while working with these classes, an early memory that shook me. I remembered making a promise. I buried my dolls and then dug them up, complete with ritual, promising I would never leave them. I had not told anyone about my forbidden games. I was about four or five.

I married early and pregnant, giving up the scholarship I had won in high school. I enjoyed my three children. They taught me with their enthusiasm and curiosity. Later, at fifty, after I had seen all three married and I thought safe and "secure," I walked away—to another job, another life.

My only daughter died four years ago from complications of a liver disease. She had lived here near me since her "secure" marriage failed. We became friends, good friends, sharing mutual challenges, facing the reality of our early relationship with each other, sharing family secrets. I had never experienced anything like the devastation and pain I felt after her death.

You talk of each loss reminding us of earlier losses. When I read your book, and even as I'm composing this letter, I feel the pain of the loss of a daughter. As I mourn for my daughter, I'm acutely aware of how hard it has been to mourn for a mother who had no skin, and remained ethereal and immortalized.

Aunts and uncles who alternately took care of me and taunted me in turn made comparisons, as they remembered their sister. "You don't look like your mother—you are dark haired, not blonde like her"; and, "Your teeth are coming in crooked; she had straight, even teeth, a great smile"; or, "Your face is freckled like a turkey egg, like your father's was. Her skin was milk white."

None of these comparisons came from Ellen Jean, my strong pioneer grandmother who said nothing and showed me how to survive. Not long ago, I found some pictures, one of me with a friend, and on the back someone had written, "She was cute as a button." I didn't know anyone ever thought that about me.

Anxiety attacks about two years after my daughter's death sent me back to therapy, for more understanding.

One among the many sentences from your book that lifted itself off the page: "But from underneath all the glitz still comes the cry of the motherless child, 'Pay attention to me!'"

The label persists. *I am a motherless child*. When I hear the title of the gospel song, I automatically add the words, "A long way from home."

A Web of Support

All roads may once have led to Rome, but in my past most roads have led from Evanston, Illinois. It was there, as a freshman at Northwestern University, where I began my search for books about early mother loss. And it was there, nine years later, that I decided to write *Motherless Daughters* after the notices I tacked up in a local café and bookstore when I was looking for other motherless women led to more phone calls than I could possibly manage. So it's perfectly appropriate that the first woman who asked me about starting a support group for motherless daughters did so at a reading in downtown Evanston when I was on my very first book tour in 1994.

I can't recall exactly what she said, and I don't think I ever got her name. But I remember that the sheet of notebook paper she passed around collected about twenty names and telephone numbers from women interested in forming a local group. The same thing happened in St. Paul, Minnesota; and in Atlanta; and Los Angeles; and Portland, Oregon; and New

York. "I came here tonight so I could sit in a room with other women like myself after years of feeling so alone," a woman in San Diego said. "But tonight isn't enough. I want to do it again and again and again."

As these women had learned, breaking through the wall and shame of silence that surrounds many motherless daughters would be only the first step toward coming to terms with their pasts. Yes, it's essential to begin talking about our losses, but we need people to talk *with*.

Since those book events in 1994, Motherless Daughters and Motherless Mothers support and social groups have started throughout the United States, from San Francisco to Denver to Detroit, and from New Orleans to Boston. The Internet has made it possible for women to reach out to each other across thousands of miles to offer comfort and hope. I've visited with groups in London and Dubai, and corresponded with group leaders based in Canada and Australia. When women cannot meet in person, they've found ways to connect in the virtual world. The Motherless Daughters group on Facebook has nearly four thousand members and offers particular support to women whose mothers have recently died. It's not unusual for a post there to receive thirty or forty responses from women who are further along on the same path.

As this book went to press, more than three dozen in-person and online groups were independently operating around the world. Many of them are listed at my web site, www.hopeedelman.com. If a group does not yet exist in your town and you'd like to start one, please read the suggestions that follow. Groups begun in a thoughtful, responsible, and consistent manner are the ones most likely to last. Motherless Daughters groups in Los Angeles, Orange County, California, and metro Detroit have been meeting for an annual luncheon on Motherless Daughters Day, the day before Mother's Day, to honor the memories of attendees' mothers, for more than fifteen years. The newest groups, in Dubuque, Iowa, and Durham, North Carolina, will hopefully persist for just as long. The friendships and bonds formed through these groups are enduring. Women coming together to help other women can be a powerful healing strategy for everyone. It's the belief upon which all of these groups have been formed.

Appendix

Starting a Motherless Daughters Support Group

Starting and running a Motherless Daughters group requires an ongoing commitment. These are some guidelines you may find helpful if you'd like to start a group in your town or online.

First, it's important to distinguish between therapeutic support groups and informal social groups. The information below can help you decide which approach is right for you.

Starting a Therapeutic Support Group

A therapeutic group will encourage all members to speak openly about their past experiences, including those that caused trauma. Sensitive material and strong emotions often come up. For this reason, it is important that therapeutic groups be led by a licensed therapist or certified health professional with experience leading such groups.

If you're not a therapeutic provider, you will take on an organizational role, starting with finding a therapist and perhaps helping to find group members. You may already know a therapist who can lead such a group. If not, local children's bereavement centers, hospices, and hospitals often have counselors who are willing to start new groups, sometimes at no cost. Private therapists may choose to charge; this is something to work out on an individual basis.

Therapeutic groups are very successful when they are time limited (say, eight or ten weeks' duration). In some cases, therapy groups have continued past this point at members' requests. There are no standardized guidelines for content or duration of the groups; this is entirely up to the counselor who leads it.

There are several ways to find members for a group. Notices in health centers, women's bookstores, clinics, and doctors' offices (especially pediatricians and ob-gyns) are often helpful. Classified ads in local publications are another option. You'll also find that word of mouth goes far.

Please be aware: In therapist-led groups, the counselor is responsible for screening potential members and deciding who is appropriate for inclusion. It is important to defer to the counselor's decisions on this matter, because counselors are trained to identify which individuals are ready for group work and which individuals might benefit from other forms of support.

Therapeutic support groups for motherless daughters tend to work best when members fit the same general criteria. For women whose loss has occurred within the past year, a bereavement group is usually more appropriate. You might want to prepare a resource list for such women, as you will probably receive some calls from daughters who've experienced a very recent death.

Age at time of loss is also important. You may find it helpful to specify a maximum age at time of loss (for example, women who were twenty and under when their mothers died). Mixing women who were young children with women who were in their late twenties does not always work well in a therapy group. The Motherless Daughters Support Groups begun in New York in the 1990s divided women into those who were ages twelve and younger and those who were teens and young adults. Although this division may not be possible in your case, be aware that losing a mother during childhood is very different from experiencing it as an adult. Not harder or easier, just different.

The same is true for women whose mothers are still living but estranged. Those who were abandoned and never saw their mothers again often experience the abandonment like a death and will often mix fine in a group of women who have lost mothers to death. This is up to the therapist's discretion. However, women whose mothers are still living but have strained relationships with them and who communicate with them even from time to time have different emotional needs. For this reason, it is not recommended that they participate in therapeutic Motherless Daughters groups with women whose mothers have died.

Starting a Motherless Daughters Social Group

These groups typically meet once or twice a month, sometimes every other month, and tend to be more like informal get-togethers. There may be a topic of discussion for each gathering, but the meetings have no formal structure. Instead, they serve as an opportunity for women to meet at someone's house or at a restaurant or local park to freely share stories and advice. A trained facilitator is not always present, but these groups work best when one or more person steps forward to act as organizer. If more than a few months pass without a gathering, these groups typically start to disband.

May social groups have started through www.meetup .com. To view them, go to the meetup.com web site, insert "Motherless Daughters" into the search engine box, and then choose "Any Distance" from the next drop-down list. The listings will show you how many women have joined each group online. You might first check to see whether a group already exists in your town. If not, and you'd like to start one this way, the procedure is fairly straightforward. Just click on "Start a Meetup Group" at the top of the home page, and follow instructions from there.

Other ways to start a social group are outlined in the section above—online postings, doctor's offices, local classified ads. You decide the parameters of the group, that is, whether it's for women who experienced both childhood and adult loss, whether abandonment will be included, and how much time should have elapsed since the loss occurred. It's less important that members of social groups fit the same criteria; some of the most successful social groups embrace all forms of mother loss. However, unlike therapeutic groups, social groups typically do not screen new members. On rare occasions someone who doesn't fit the criteria for your group or someone who is acting inappropriately toward others will need to be asked to leave the group. For this reason, it can be very helpful to have a co-organizer to consult with and who can back you up.

Women have reported that the community and friendships they encounter through such groups become vital and sustaining forces in all areas of their lives. If you would like

to list your group on the "Support Groups" page at www
.hopeedelman.com, please send an email to hopeedelman@
gmail.com that includes all necessary information, including
your contact information.

Best of luck to you in your venture!

The information provided here is neither an endorsement of any group that has formed or
will form nor an official statement of guidelines. The author and publisher cannot be held
responsible for anything that occurs surrounding the formation of such a group or for the
outcome of any related or subsequent meetings.

Sources and Resources

Bidwell Smith, Claire. *The Rules of Inheritance*. New York: Plume, 2012.

Davidman, Lynn. *Motherloss*. Berkeley: University of California Press, 2000.

Granot, Tamar. *Without You*. Philadelphia: Jessica Kingsley, 2005.

Harris, Maxine. *The Loss That Is Forever*. New York: Plume, 1995.

Joseph, Stephen. *What Doesn't Kill Us*. New York: Basic Books, 2011.

Kaplan, Louise J. *No Voice Is Ever Wholly Lost*. New York: Simon & Schuster, 1995.

Lauck, Jennifer. *Blackbird*. New York: Pocket Books, 2000.

O'Fallon, Margaret, and Margaret Vaillancourt, eds. *Kiss Me Goodnight*. St. Paul, MN: Syren, 2005.

O'Rourke, Meghan. *The Long Goodbye*. New York: Riverhead, 2012.

Rando, Therese A. *How to Go On Living When Someone You Love Dies*. New York: Bantam, 1991.

Romm, Robin. *The Mercy Papers*. New York: Scribner, 2009.

Silverman, Phyllis Rolfe. *Never Too Young to Know*. New York: Oxford University Press, 1999.

Strayed, Cheryl. *Wild*. New York: Vintage, 2013.

Vincent, Erin. *Grief Girl*. New York: Ember, 2008.

Viorst, Judith. *Necessary Losses*. New York: Fawcett Gold Medal, 1987.

Volkan, Vamik D., and Elizabeth Zintl. *Life After Loss: The Lessons of Grief*. New York: Scribner's, 1993.

Worden, J. William. *Children and Grief*. New York: Guilford Press, 1996.

Index

Made in the USA
Las Vegas, NV
12 December 2020